THOMAS MERTON:
MASTER OF ATTENTION

THOMAS MERTON: MASTER OF ATTENTION

An Exploration of Prayer

ROBERT WALDRON

PAULIST PRESS
New York/Mahwah, N.J.

This edition by arrangement with
Darton, Longman and Todd Ltd
1 Spencer Court
140–142 Wandsworth High Street
London SW18 4JJ

ISBN 978-0-8091-4521-8

Library of Congress Control Number: 2007939506

Published in 2008 by
PAULIST PRESS
997 Macarthur Boulevard
Mahwah, New Jersey 07430

Phototypeset by YHT Ltd, London

Printed and bound in Great Britain

CONTENTS

ACKNOWLEDGEMENTS

Deepest gratitude to Sandra Walter for her superb editing of my book from its inception to its final form. I also wish to thank John Hart for all his encouragement during the writing of my book. A special thank you to Darton, Longman and Todd's Brendan Walsh, who seriously considered an e-mail from America, which led to my writing *Thomas Merton: Master of Attention*. I also wish to thank my editor at DLT, Helen Porter and also Claudine Nightingale, the first person I contacted at DLT, who noted my e-mail and passed it on.

The author and publisher are grateful for permission to reproduce the following copyright material:

'I always obey my nurse' by Thomas Merton, from *Eighteen Poems*, copyright © 1977, 1985 by The Trustees of the Merton Legacy Trust. Reprinted by permission of New Directions Publishing Corp. Sales Territory: UK & British Commonwealth only.

Excerpts by Thomas Merton from *The Asian Journal of Thomas Merton*, copyright © 1975 by The Trustees of the Merton Legacy Trust. Reprinted by permission of New Directions Publishing Corp. Sales Territory: UK & British Commonwealth only.

Excerpts from *A Vow of Conversation: Journals 1964–1965* by Thomas Merton. Copyright © 1988 by the Merton Legacy Trust. Reprinted by permission of Farrar, Straus and Giroux, LLC.

Excerpts from *The Sign of Jonas* by Thomas Merton. Copyright © 1953 by The Abbey of Gethsemani. Reprinted by permission of Curtis Brown, Ltd. Territory: UK.

Excerpts from *Waiting for God* by Simone Weil translated by Emma Craufurd, copyright © 1951, renewed 1979 by G.P.

Putnam's Sons. *US*: used by permission of G.P. Putnam's Sons, a division of Penguin Group (USA) Inc. *UK and Canada*: used by permission of Sanford J. Greenburger Associates, 55 5th Avenue, New York.

Attention

(inspired by Simone Weil)

Lord,
Teach me to be attentive
To all your vestiges:
To the first light,
To the waking bird,
To the leaf's rustle and the rain's drop,
To the scent of water and the sky's hue
And the rise of the wind;
Lord,
Teach me to be so attentive that
I shall hear the first flakes of the snow's fall.

Robert Waldron

INTRODUCTION

You may well ask, 'Why another book about Thomas Merton?' He is perhaps one of the most written-about spiritual figures of the twentieth century. Ever since the publication of his best-selling autobiography *The Seven Storey Mountain*, Merton has been at the forefront of modern spirituality; read, studied and emulated. He could have served as the model for Carl Jung's *Modern Man in Search of a Soul*. And the good news is that he found his soul, the result of individuation, God's grace and his mastering of the art of attention.

I have written three books about Merton. Each was an attempt to understand more deeply the man who sacrificed everything to pursue 'GOD ALONE' (written above the Abbey of Gethsemani's entrance) in the silence and solitude of an abbey located in the remote hills of Kentucky – a medieval life that was the antithesis of Merton's life in New York City, the intellectual and artistic center of America, where he lived as a student, teacher and writer.

Each of my books approached Merton from a different perspective. My first book, *Thomas Merton in Search of His Soul,* analysed Merton's life by employing the paradigm of Jung's theory of individuation, one that yielded useful psychological insights about why he had chosen monastic life and why he remained a monk. The second, *Poetry as Prayer: Thomas Merton,* entailed an effort to understand Merton the poet; Merton always viewed himself first and foremost as a poet, and although many think his first published book was his famous memoir, it was actually a book of verse, *Thirty Poems* (1944). Between 1944–9, Merton wrote four books of poetry. My third, *Walking with Thomas Merton, Discovering His Poetry, Essays and Journals,* was more general in its scope. I studied Merton's journals and essays, searching for the secret of his spiritual life as well as the source of his commitment to monastic life during a time when many of his post-Vatican II brothers and sisters abandoned their vocations to return to secular life.

After writing these books, I still had not solved the enigma of Merton, and I doubt anyone ever will. When I was recently at a crossroad in my spiritual life, feeling particularly perplexed and lost when it came to prayer, I again returned to Merton only to be reminded that although he has important things to say about prayer, he invariably speaks about it in the abstract, offering no methodology. His avoidance of schema clearly indicates that he never wished to appear as if he had found the one and only successful technique of prayer. In fact, he was more inclined toward the oriental idea that suggests that the one who knows (enlightened) remains silent.

At the time, I was simultaneously reading Merton and Simone Weil when after another reading of my favorite of Merton's journals, *A Vow of Conversation*, I finally realized that although he denied having a method of prayer, Merton had indeed lived his life by method, although I prefer the word 'way' instead of 'method,' which implies something coldly mechanistic. His 'way' can be summarized by one word: attention. Merton's prayer life was congruent, I discovered, with Simone Weil's theory of prayer, one she summarizes in a sentence, 'Absolutely unmixed attention is prayer.'[1]

As a teacher of English literature, I had been engaged in literary exegesis for over thirty years, never directly linking what I read and taught to prayer. After reading Weil's essay 'Reflections on the right use of school studies with a view to the love of God', a whole new world of prayer opened for me, and I discovered that my years of close readings of texts like *King Lear*, *Hamlet*, *Antigone*, *Portrait of an Artist as a Young Man* and *Murder in the Cathedral* as well as scores of poems, had, without my realizing it, been prayer. Weil writes:

> The key to a Christian conception of studies is the realization that prayer consists of attention. It is the orientation of all the attention of which the soul is capable toward God. The quality of the attention counts for much in the quality of the prayer. Warmth of heart cannot make up for it. The highest part of the attention only makes contact with God, when prayer is

intense and pure enough for such a contact to be established;
but the whole attention is turned toward God.[2]

Living attentively had become so much a part of Merton's life that I
was reminded of Zen calligraphists: when engaged in calligraphy, a
Buddhist monk enters an exquisitely attentive zone, his whole
being focused on the act of creation, forgetting himself only to
return to himself to find, as if for the first time, what he has created.
In his posthumously published journal *A Vow of Conversation*, we
see Merton at his attentive best, a monk happy, creative and at
peace. He gradually moves into his hermitage, at first staying only
the days but gradually the nights until he becomes a fulltime resident; it was the serenest period of his life. He has become the
opposite of the smug, narrow-minded triumphalist Catholic convert of *The Seven Storey Mountain*, a man disdainful of the world,
and of non-Catholics. The monk of the hermitage is a world-
embracing, compassionate, wise, tolerant man, solicitously reaching
out to the world with his poems, essays, and books on spirituality.

Credit for this transformation must in part be given to his formation within the context of traditional monasticism with its
asceticism, its vows, and its Rule of St Benedict, but there were
other factors that rendered him able to transcend strict Cistercian
conditioning, allowing him to become more flexible, to open
himself to other religions, other ways of thinking, especially that of
Zen Buddhism with its ultimate aim the diminishment of ego and
the cultivation of direct seeing.

With Weil's definition of prayer in mind, I understood for the
first time how Merton had become, to use Lawrence Cunning-
ham's phrase, a 'spiritual master.' Merton, of course, prayed in
church while chanting the psalms, when attending and later celebrating Mass, and at set times during the day he meditated on
biblical texts. But he also prayed while reading, studying and
writing, while sweeping and cleaning his hermitage, while
watching the deer outside his door, while gazing upon the Kentucky hills or listening to the birds outside his window, while
looking at the blazing fire in his hearth on cold winter days and
nights. His whole life was emblematic of a blooming flower,
reaching its fullest flowering when he was a hermit, a time when
Merton experienced his deepest silence and greatest solitude.

I had for a short time thought I was unique in finding the connection between Merton and Weil until I read Nobel laureate Czeslaw Milosz's encomium to the two spiritual writers. He writes:

> The 20th century remains for us a century of great criminals, yet also of a few bright figures, whose creative thought may tip the scales of victory of good over evil. Among them I see Simone Weil and Albert Camus, and Thomas Merton as well.[3]

How fitting that they now are linked forever, these two God-seekers who had never known they worshipped at the same church, Corpus Christi in New York City, and had been counseled by the same man, Doctor Tom Bennett, Merton's godfather and guardian, and Weil's doctor in London where she died. Merton and Weil had both experienced Christ in the 1930s, Merton while visiting Rome's great basilicas, and Simone Weil while listening to Gregorian chant and liturgy during a visit with her mother to the French monastery of Solesme. Merton was captured by the haunting beauty of the Byzantine mosaics of Christ; he writes, 'For the first time in my whole life I began to find out something of who this Person was that men call Christ ... It is the Christ of the Apocalypse, the Christ of the Martyrs, the Christ of the Father ... It is Christ King.'[4]

At Solesme, Weil spent ten days, from Palm Sunday to Easter Tuesday, attending the liturgical services. She writes:

> I was suffering from splitting headaches, each sound hurt me like a blow; by an extreme effort of concentration I was able to rise above this wretched flesh, to leave it to suffer by itself, heaped up in a corner, and to find a pure and perfect joy in the unimaginable beauty of the chanting and the words. This experience enabled me by analogy to get a better understanding of the possibility of loving divine love in the midst of affliction. It goes without saying that in the course of these services the thought of the Passion of Christ entered into my being once and for all.[5]

Weil also met an Oxford graduate, whose face appeared so radiant after receiving Holy Communion, she never forgot it. She later became friendly with him; she writes:

> For he told me of the existence of those English poets of the seventeenth century who are named metaphysical. In reading them later on, I discovered the poem of which I read you what is unfortunately a very inadequate translation. It is called 'Love.' I learned it by heart. Often at the culminating point of a violent headache, I make myself say it over, concentrating all my attention upon it and clinging with all my soul to the tenderness it enshrines. I used to think I was merely reciting it as a beautiful poem, but without my knowing it the recitation had the virtue of a prayer. It was during one of these recitations that, as I told you, Christ himself came down and took possession of me.[6]

These two mystics found Christ through aesthetics: by their attention to the beauty of Christ as expressed in art: Byzantine mosaics, Gregorian chant and poetry. Although it would take many years for Merton to articulate his theory of beauty, Weil had early on formed her theories about the dynamic import of attention to beauty. She writes:

> In everything which gives us the pure authentic feeling of beauty there is really the presence of God. There is, as it were, an incarnation of God in the world, and it is indicated by beauty. The beautiful is the experimental proof that the incarnation is possible. Hence all art of the highest order is religious in essence. (That is what people have forgotten today.) A Gregorian melody is as powerful a witness as the death of a martyr.[7]

Like Merton, Weil had taught language (as well as history). It was in the classroom that her theory of attention first surfaced. She writes:

> The authentic and pure values – truth, beauty and goodness – in the activity of a human being are the results of one and the same act, a certain application of the full attention to the

object. Teaching should have no aim but to prepare, by training the attention, for the possibility of such an act.[8]

When he entered the Abbey of Gethsemani, Merton was already capable of acute attention: the son of an accomplished painter, he possessed a connoisseur's eye for beauty; he also wrote poetry and novels, read voraciously and had taught English at Columbia and St Bonaventure College. Such activities demand acute powers of attention. And they held him in good stead when he became a monk, shifting his attention from literature and art to *lectio divina*. His acutely appreciative eye for artistic beauty lay quiescent now that he no longer had access to museums and art galleries, as well as his artistic friends. It was not a period of total loss, however, for Merton's abbey was located in a particularly beautiful part of Kentucky, and he daily feasted his eye on nature's beauty.

As a monk at the Abbey of Gethsemani, Merton would have ample opportunity to sharpen his reading skills, for the kind of formal prayer required of him in his formation was meditation, based upon the reading and pondering of *lectio divina*: holy reading.

What is *lectio divina*? It is primarily the reading of the Scriptures. Trappist monks chant the complete psalter every two weeks. There are also Bible readings, both private and public. For private reading there are various methods. Merton practiced them all. And we shall see how they honed his powers of attention, allowing him to progress in prayer, although he would be the last one to actually use the word progress. He writes: 'how to make progress' is a good way to make people too aware of themselves.[9]

During the first fifteen years of Merton's life as a monk, there was little opportunity to offer his attention to the visual arts. He surely appreciated the beauty of nature, and his journals are fraught with lyrical descriptions of the rural environs of Gethsemani. When he became a hermit in the mid-1960s, his interest in art again blossomed as he began to take up brush and ink to practice calligraphy. He became quite an accomplished calligrapher, calligraphy another way of prayer for Merton, teaching him to lose himself, to see again, and to create art both astonishingly fresh and modern, art he humbly described as graffiti, but it was much more than that; his calligraphies were signs of 'obscure reconciliations and agreements.'[10] Such art was only possible to Merton the hermit, who had learned from Zen that the artist has to become empty and disappear. And as Weil repeatedly says in her writing, the way to become empty is to become attentive.

As Merton matured as a monk, he struggled with his life's dominant question, 'What is contemplation?' He had written several books grappling with this question. But truly to understand what he meant by contemplation, it is best to look at his life, especially his life as a hermit, for the answer to his question is found in *how* he lived. And we shall look closely at his hermitage years, for it is during this time that Merton embodied contemplation, living at an exquisite pitch of attention.

When he attempts to verbalise his thoughts on prayer, it is surprising how much he sounds like Simone Weil, with the word 'attentive' dominating his articulations. No doubt about it, Merton understood that prayer is an act of attention; therefore, it is an activity that can be cultivated and improved, not so much by method but by acute acts of seeing.

In conclusion, the purpose of this book is two-fold; first, to offer a new perspective of Merton and his prayer life, second, to encourage people not to give up on prayer: deep prayer is not an esoteric activity meant only for mystics and proficients: it is available to all of us, if we would only pay attention.

By offering our attention to Merton, we shall perhaps fulfill Plato's dictum, 'We become what we behold' – and like Merton, we too will become more prayerful and more Christ-like.

BIOGRAPHY

Thomas Merton was born on 31 January 1915 in Prades, France, to an American mother with Quaker leanings and a New Zealander father, a member of the Church of England. In 1921, when Tom was six, his mother died of cancer. In one of the most touching scenes in his autobiography, *The Seven Storey Mountain*, the boy Merton sits alone inside a rain-splattered car, while his father enters the hospital for his last visit with his wife. Later, the boy receives a letter from his mother, her final farewell to her son.

Thereafter, Merton was raised in turn by either his grandparents or his father. In 1928, leaving behind his younger son John Paul with his maternal grandparents on Long Island, Owen Merton and his teenage son Tom moved to France, settling in St Antonin. Merton often watched his father paint the French landscape; he once observed that his father painted like Cézanne, which tells us as much about Owen Merton as it does about his son, a youngster already gifted with an eye for beauty. Both eventually left St Antonin for England where Merton attended Oakham in Rutland, a boarding school with a solid reputation, and there his flair for languages won him a scholarship to Clare College at the University of Cambridge.

Merton attended Cambridge for a year without academically distinguishing himself, partly due to his father's death from brain cancer in 1931. Unsupervised as an undergraduate at Cambridge, Merton fell into a life of partying, dating and drinking; he had inadvertently become a member of an exclusive club that would notoriously be described as the 'lost generation.' When guardian, Tom Bennett, learned that Merton had fathered a child, he suggested that Merton leave England to begin again in America, for his libertine-like behaviour would be unlikely to procure him a job in the British Civil Service, Merton's original plan. He departed England to live with his maternal grandparents in Long

Island, and later, in February, 1935, he enrolled at Columbia University.

At first, Columbia was an exciting place for Merton both socially and intellectually. At the same time, however, he remained an agnostic, hostile to formal religion even after a profound spiritual experience in Rome when he was eighteen. His shame for his dissolute life at Cambridge had marked him with a nagging sense of guilt, from which he found relief in a frenetic lifestyle, a destructive pattern beginning all over again at Columbia in a whirl of drinking, dating and frequenting jazz dives, all of which failed to assuage a growing sense of life's emptiness.

Glimpsing Etienne Gilson's *The Spirit of Medieval Philosophy* in Scribner's window, he impulsively purchased it. Gilson introduced him to a concept of God that he found intellectually satisfying: God is not enraged, autocratically intent upon condemning as many people as possible; rather, God is loving and compassionate, the kind of God Merton desperately needed to believe in for only such a God, he felt, could cleanse his soul of corruption.

Merton had also read widely in poetry: Dante, William Blake and Gerard Manley Hopkins. When Merton was a boy of ten, his father had him read William Blake's poetry. Tom's love of Blake would never fade, and he would write his master's thesis on the great poet. As for Dante, Merton confessed in his autobiography that the only goodness he experienced at Cambridge was his introduction to Dante's *The Divine Comedy*. Merton also fell in love with the rhapsodic Jesuit poet Gerard Manley Hopkins, and while at Columbia he read an account of Hopkins' conversion to Catholicism through the influence of John Henry Newman. This became the inspiration for Merton to take instruction to become a Christian. On 18 November 1938 he was baptised at Corpus Christi Church in New York City.

In conversion fervor, Merton purchased the works of St John of the Cross. He also read St Teresa of Avila's *Autobiography*, St Augustine's *Confessions* and St Ignatius of Loyola's *Spiritual Exercises*, profound spiritual fare for one so new to spirituality.

While teaching English at the Franciscan's St Bonaventure College in Olean, New York, Merton came to admire Franciscan simplicity, poverty and joy. He was tentatively accepted into the Order, only later to have them rescind their offer. In a burst of scrupulosity, he confessed to the Franciscans his dissolute ways at Cambridge as well as his fathering a child. At first, he was devastated by the rejection, but in 1941, at the recommendation of Dan Walsh, Merton's friend and also part time philosophy teacher at Columbia, Merton spent Holy Week at the Abbey of Gethsemani in Kentucky. He was astonished by its holy ambience, writing in his journal, 'This is the center of America.' He applied for admission and was accepted, warts and all.

On 10 December 1941 he entered the Cistercian Order, and three days later he became a postulant choir monk with one desire: to disappear into God. The ideal of the Cistercian (also called Trappist) is aimed at stripping all that impedes union with God, buttressed by vows of obedience, chastity and poverty. Only when false selves have been uprooted and discarded will emerge the True Self who is Christ, 'Not I but Christ in me.' This Christ-transformation became Merton's *raison d'être*. He writes, 'The work of recovery of this lost likeness is effected by stripping away all that is alien and foreign to our true selves.'[1]

Merton's life as a monk was a medieval one of silence, solitude, asceticism and prayer known as *lectio divina*. Choir monks, dressed in white robes and black scapulars, devoted their days to the ancient, Benedictine dictum, *ora et labora* (prayer and work). It was a difficult and demanding life, but for Merton it was heaven on earth: the boy who had been an orphan at sixteen was now a man who had at last found his true home and his life's purpose: to save his soul.

At the Abbey of Gethsemani, Merton slept in a long dormitory divided into cells by partitions with only a curtain for a door, allowing little privacy. Each cell contained a wooden bed frame with a straw mattress, a crucifix, and a stoup for holy water. The monks' diet was vegetarian, meat forbidden but fish and eggs permitted. During the holy seasons of Advent and Lent, the community fasted more strictly. The schedule Merton followed in 1941 is as follows:

2:00 a.m.	Rise, followed by choir for Matins and Lauds
2:30 a.m.	Meditation
3:00 a.m.	Night Office
5:30 a.m.	Prime followed by Chapter

7:45 a.m.	Tierce, High Mass, Sext
11:30 a.m.	Dinner
4:30 p.m.	Vespers
5:30 p.m.	Collation (light refreshment)
6:10 p.m.	Compline and the singing of Salve Regina
7:00 p.m.	Retire

In 1948, Merton's autobiography *The Seven Storey Mountain* was published. No one had predicted its now legendary success; in the first year alone it sold over 600,000 hardback copies. Thus was launched Thomas Merton's career both as a spiritual writer and spiritual master. A year later Merton wrote *Seeds of Contemplation*, also a best-seller, introducing his readers to the practice of contemplation. The weary postsecond world war generation was hungry for such a book which promised both peace of soul and a deeper inner life in God.

The 1950s saw Merton's publication of more than a dozen books and a host of essays and reviews. In 1953, he published his popular journal, *The Sign of Jonas*, and in 1955 appeared *No Man Is an Island*. He also continued his study of Buddhism, corresponding with D. Suzuki, the leading Zen Buddhist intellectual of the time. Merton received permission from his abbot to visit Suzuki in the early 1960s, a meeting Merton would treasure for the rest of his life, for in Suzuki Merton had finally met a Zen man radiant with the wisdom of the East.

On 18 March 1956 Merton traveled to Louisville, Kentucky where he experienced his now famous 'Louisville Vision.' Standing on the corner of Fourth and Walnut Streets, he observed the busy crowd:

> In Louisville, at the corner of Fourth and Walnut, in the center of the shopping district, I was suddenly overwhelmed with the realization that I loved all those people, that they were mine and I theirs, that we could not be alien to one another even though we were total strangers. It was like waking from a dream of separateness, of spurious self-isolation in a special world of renunciation and supposed holiness. The whole illusion of separate holy existence is a dream .... Thank God, thank God that I am like other men, that I am only a man among others. [2]

This realization marked a turning point in his life. Whereas the first fifteen years of his monastic life were marked by the inner gaze, attention focused primarily on *lectio divina* and issues that could only be described as 'in-house,' Merton now developed an outer gaze, one focused on the world and its suffering. Merton, who fled the world in disdain, viewing it as fraught with evil, now embraced it in compassion. This shift, I believe, was the result of his practice of attention, to be addressed later.

And then the most singular event of his monastic life: he was allowed to become a hermit, to live in a hermitage within the enclosure of the Abbey of Gethsemani. On the Feast of Saint Bernard, 1965, Merton took full occupation of the cinder block building, his *locus Dei* for the remainder of his life.

The hermitage years were busy ones for Merton. He reached out to other religions in his writings with the hope that such dialogue would contribute to world unity and peace. He published several books on his abiding interest in Zen, including *Mystics and Zen Masters* (1967) and *Zen and the Birds of Appetite* (1968), as well as his 'renderings' of the Chinese sage, Chuang Tzu, *The Way of Chuang Tzu* (1965). He also wrote a number of books addressing political issues: *Seeds of Destruction*, *Gandhi on Non-Violence* (editor), *Raids on the Unspeakable*, and *Faith and Violence*.

Merton had hoped that the move into the hermitage would protect and ensure his silence and solitude. But anyone reading his journals will discover that people sought him for any number of things, and he counted among his visitors some of the world's famous: folk singer Joan Baez, poet Denise Levertov, Nobel laureate Czeslaw Milosz, theologian Jacque Maritain, publisher James Laughlin, poet Brother Antoninus, writer/photographer John Howard Griffin, and many others. And it should be mentioned that he indeed missed communal life, often feeling lonely in his hermitage, its edge blunted by following a strict schedule from his rising at 2:15 a.m. to his retiring at 7:00 p.m.

While living at the hermitage, Merton received an invitation to travel to Bangkok, Thailand, to speak at a world conference on the Eastern and Western monastic experience. Merton had long been fascinated by Asian spirituality, having become a known and respected expert on Buddhism and Taoism.

In the East, Merton experienced a profound epiphanic moment

while standing before the huge stone Buddhas of Polonnaruwa. He writes, 'Looking at these figures, I was suddenly, almost forcibly, jerked clean out of the habitual, half-tied vision of things. An inner clearness, clarity, as if exploding from the rocks themselves, became evident and oblivious.'[3] Kipling had once said that the East and the West would never meet. As he stood in his bare feet before the Buddhas, the Trappist monk, Thomas Merton, had surely proved him wrong.

Had his epiphany been a momentary *satori* (enlightenment)? Merton personally felt that a Christian could, just as a Buddhist, experience *satori*. But I am inclined to believe that Merton experienced a greater integration, a greater wholeness – holiness, if you will. Merton describes the integrated person:

> He apprehends his life fully and wholly from an inner ground that is at once more universal than the empirical ego and yet entirely his own. He is in a certain sense 'cosmic' and 'universal man.' He has attained a deeper, fuller identity than that of his limited ego-self, which is only a fragment of his being. He is in a certain sense identified with everybody.[4]

In Bangkok, on 10 December 1968 (the twenty-seventh anniversary of his entry into Gethsemani), Merton delivered his final talk at the world conference, a paper titled 'Marxism and monastic perspectives,' focused on the transformation of the self as the goal of the monastic journey, both East and West. He then retired to his room. Later, emerging from a shower, he inadvertently contacted a faulty fan near his bed and was electrocuted by 220 volts of power. His body was later found and soon flown back to America on a plane returning home the bodies of American soldiers killed in the Vietnam War, a sad irony, for Merton had opposed this war in his writing, a political position alienating many conservative pro-war Catholics.

Thomas Merton lies buried in the monks' cemetery at the Abbey of Gethsemani.

THE CONNOISSEUR OF BEAUTY

Like his mother, Merton's father battled cancer for several years, and on at least two occasions, he asked his son to pray for him. When his father was admitted to hospital in London Merton writes:

> One day I found his bed covered with little sheets of blue notepaper on which he had been drawing. And the drawings were *real drawings*. But they were unlike anything he had ever done before – pictures of little, *irate Byzantine-looking* saints with beards and great halos.[1] (my emphasis)

Notice that young Merton renders an artistic judgement about his father's drawings: they are 'real drawings,' i.e. they are not scribbles, doodles, or worthless scraps but serious artistic creations. Not for nothing had the young Merton traipsed after his father on excursions to Provincetown, Bermuda, France and Scotland, an education in art unto itself. The drawings are numinous portraits of saints with halos, but the word 'irate' suggests that on a deep level Owen Merton was involved in a spiritual struggle; or else the young Merton had psychologically projected onto the images his unconscious anger about his father's illness and imminent death.

Merton described his father as a man of faith, and that behind the 'walls of isolation, his intelligence and his will, unimpaired, and not hampered in any essential way by the partial obstruction of some of his senses, were turned to God, and communed with God who was with him and in him, and who gave him, as I believe, light to understand and to make use of his suffering for his own good, and to perfect his soul.'[2] Byzantine saints: what a gift to his son, who shortly would have one of his life's great spiritual epiphanies involving the exquisite beauty of Byzantine mosaics in Rome. The life and death of Merton's father would forever remain an integral part of Merton's spiritual journey.

On 18 January 1931, just after he returned from his Christmas trip to Strasbourg, Tom learned about his father's death when Oakham's headmaster handed him a telegram with the devastating news. Barely sixteen, Merton was now an orphan.

Owen Merton had appointed his friend Dr Tom Bennett as his son's guardian. Bennett, a cultured man, introduced young Merton to writers like Joyce, Hemingway and D.H. Lawrence as well as to painters like Chagall, their opinions differing, however, on modernists like Picasso, an artist Merton greatly admired. When Merton visited Bennett and his wife Iris at their elegant London flat, he lived a life of luxury, being served breakfast in bed by a French maid.

Back at Oakham, Merton studied diligently. When he won a scholarship to Clare College, Cambridge University, Tom Bennett escorted young Merton to London's Café Anglais to celebrate his success as well as his eighteenth birthday. The next day Merton set off for a continental holiday. His time spent in Rome would be the turning point of his young life.

In Rome, bored after touring its many ruins, Merton started to visit Rome's religious shrines, fascinated by their Byzantine mosaics, both stunningly beautiful and mysteriously uplifting. He eagerly sped from church to church to gaze at their art as well as their holy relics hidden within their doors, aisles and arches. Gazing upon the iconic splendor of mosaics and stained glass windows, he became more and more enthralled by their haunting beauty and soon realized that he had inadvertently become a pilgrim, one seeking spiritual peace.

But it was to the huge icons of Christ, in particular, that he always returned:

> And now for the first time in my life I began to find out something of Who this Person was that men called Christ. It was obscure, but it was a true knowledge of Him, in some sense, truer than I knew and truer than I would admit. But it was in Rome that my conception of Christ was formed. It was there I first saw Him, Whom I now serve as my God and my king, and Who owns and rules my life.[3]

To learn about Jesus Christ, still a mysterious figure to Merton, he purchased a Vulgate Bible to read and study; however, his actual rebirth in the waters of Christian baptism remained several years away. But through the beauty of art, God had touched him, and he would never again be the same person. Surely the opening of one of his most popular books reflects back on what happened to him in Rome:

> Every moment and every event of every man's life on earth plants something in his soul. For just as the wind carries thousands of invisible and visible winged seeds, to the stream of time brings with it germs of spiritual vitality that come to rest imperceptibly in the minds and wills of men. Most of these unnumbered seeds perish and are lost, because men are not prepared to receive them: for such seeds as these can not spring up anywhere except in the good soul of liberty and desire.[4]

He found a 'kind of interior peace'[5] in the great basilicas, and for the first time he felt not like an interloper but as someone who belonged. No doubt Christ had touched Merton via beauty. Simone Weil writes:

> The beauty of the world is Christ's tender smile for us coming through matter. He is really present in the universal beauty. The love of this beauty proceeds from God dwelling in our souls and goes out to God present in the universe. It also is like a sacrament.[6]

If, at the time, someone had suggested to Merton that looking at art was prayer, he might have disagreed, although gradually he would come to a similar conclusion. More of that later.

What remains factual is that his attention to the beauty of the Byzantine mosaics was so intense that he moved beyond aesthetics into an experience of transformation, one founded upon the transcendence of ego. Merton writes:

> Art enables us to find ourselves and lose ourselves at the same time. The mind that responds to the intellectual and spiritual values that lie hidden in a poem, a painting, or a piece of music,

discovers a spiritual vitality that lifts it above itself, takes it out of itself, and makes it present to itself on a level of being that it did not know it could ever achieve.[7]

The theologian John Navone supports Merton's concept of art's power over the soul. He writes:

> Beauty is at the heart of all human motivation. True beauty as the attractiveness of the truly good motivates human life and development in that intellectual, moral, and religious self-transcendence that constitutes human authenticity or excellence.
>
> Without our experiencing the attractiveness or beauty of intellectual, moral and religious goods, such goods are bereft of their power to transform our lives. Beauty is the enabling power of the truly good to draw us out of ourselves for the achievement of excellence.[8]

In Rome, God had lured Merton to him, with beauty as bait, although complete capture would still be several years away. That God employs snares to win us to Him is a pivotal aspect of Weil's theory of beauty. She writes, 'The soul's natural inclination to love beauty is the trap God most frequently uses in order to win it and open it to the breath from on high.'[9]

Shortly after viewing the Byzantine icons, Merton sensed his father's presence in his hotel room on the corner of Via Sistina and Via Tritone. He writes one of the most haunting passages in modern twentieth-century memoirs:

> Suddenly it seemed to me that Father, who had now been dead more than a year, was there with me. The sense of his presence was as vivid and as real and as startling as if he had touched my arm or spoken to me. The whole thing passed in a flash, but in that flash, instantly, I was overwhelmed with a sudden and profound insight into the misery and corruption of my own soul, and I was pierced deeply with a light that made me realize something of the condition I was in, and I was filled with horror at what I saw, and my whole being rose up in revolt against what was within me, and my soul desired escape

and liberation and freedom from all this with an intensity and an urgency unlike anything I had ever known before.[10]

Merton's admitting, 'I was pierced deeply with a light' is the language of the mystics. We need only recall Bernini's sculpture of *The Ecstasy of St Teresa.* Walter Hilton describes such illumination in his *The Scale of Perfection:* 'He openeth the inner eyes of the soul when He lighteneth the reason through touching of His blessed light, for to see Him and know Him; not all fully at once, but little and little by divers times, as the soul may suffer him.'[11]

The message of his father's Hamlet-like visitation is loud and clear: 'Son, you're wasting your life.' And Merton for the first time throws himself into self-forgetting prayer:

> And now for the first time in my whole life I really began to pray – praying not with my lips and with my intellect and my imagination, but praying out of the very roots of my life and of my being, and praying to the God I had never known, to reach down towards me out of his darkness and to help me to get free of the thousand terrible things that held my will in their slavery.[12]

Merton's prayer is not one of repeating words, or one of intellect or even imagination. He loses himself in something totally Other, a praying that is imageless; it is clear that he has for the first time experienced contemplation, a word he likely at this point in his life knew little about. But contemplation would become the dominant pursuit of his life. As with most of us, his prayer life began with 'my lips' – vocal prayers like the 'Our Father' he learned at his grandmother's knee – and then later intellect would take over, prayer like meditation, the musing upon biblical passages, to be followed by imaginative prayer like St Ignatius of Loyola's method of composition of place. But the kind of prayer that involved self-loss in the 'darkness' of God is contemplation, the prayer of the mystic.

Mystical prayer has nothing to do with words and petitions, of what is commonly considered prayer. It is not articulate; it has no form. It is, in the words of a medieval English mystic, 'naught else but a yearning of soul,' wherein the soul is united to God in its ground without the intervention of imagination or reason or of anything but a simple attention of the mind and a humble self-forgetting action of the will.[13] Or, so he would think for many years until he realized that contemplation was not an esoteric kind of prayer meant only for proficients but for everyone. As a monk Merton's primary purpose in his writing was to teach ordinary people about contemplation, to assure them that it was also accessible to them.

At twenty-four, Merton was well established in New York City, teaching English at Columbia and later at St Bonaventure at Olean, New York. At the World's Fair (1939), he viewed paintings by Fra Angelico, El Greco, Bruegel, and Bosch. An astute critic of art, Merton was confident in his judgements, and not the least shy about revealing his likes and dislikes in his journal. Merton's appraisal, for instance, of Fra Angelico's *Temptation of Saint Anthony* is appreciatively exact and penetrating:

> Completely perfect composition. The figure of the Saint's a little left of center of the picture, caught in a kind of slow dancing movement away from a leaf on the dry ground, the only thing that seems to be tempting him. Perfect movement of the drapery, a black cassock, and kind of luminous deep gray cloak: his face: not much less melancholy serenity than that of an ancient Greek statue. Behind, a bright red church on a hill: some towers against a perfectly luminous sky – a line of trees with enameled, dark foliage. Sharp outlines of the brilliant, pure-colored fantastic landscape around him.[14]

An established art critic could not have done a better job of describing this painting. Merton examines its beauty, its composition, its technique and its nuances. His looking becomes an act of pure attention. Nothing escapes his attention: the slow movement of a single leaf on a dry ground; the drapery of the black cassock, the gray cloak, the description of the Saint's face, and the bright red church on a hill. Even the trees' foliage is described. His vision requires no cleansing: here is a young man who knows *how* to look.

One thinks of Aldous Huxley's book *The Doors of Perception* in which Huxley narrates his use of the drug mescalin, hoping to produce a new mode of consciousness, allowing him, in particular, to intensify his visual experiences into a 'sacramental vision of reality.' Merton, it seems, needs no such stimulant. In fact, Merton would later gently chide Huxley for encouraging people to take drugs, arguing that the doors of perception can be kept clean by safe, time-honored methods, e.g. the practice of meditation.

Simone Weil taught that what was important, regardless of whether or not one found God, was the act of looking and waiting with open eyes: 'Looking is what saves us.'[15](An echo of Dostoevsky's 'Beauty will save the world'). Salvation, she says, lies not in possessing or consuming or controlling, but watching, waiting, expecting nothing, surrendering all. And when it came to art, like paintings and music, Weil says:

> Every true artist has had real, direct, and immediate contact with the beauty of the world, contact that is of the nature of a sacrament. God has inspired every first rate work of art, though its subject may be utterly and entirely secular.[16]

Merton, as had Weil, realized that the kind of looking he practiced at the World's Fair was similar to praying; at the end of his commentary on Fra Angelico, he writes, 'Looking at this picture is exactly the same sort of thing as praying.'[17] His comment echoes Weil's 'Absolutely unmixed attention is prayer.'[18] How amazing that this man and woman would come to a similar conclusion about the 'simple' act of attentive looking, and at roughly the same time, the 1930s.

Weil's definition of prayer is a provocative one. Note the staggering number of books published every year on 'How to Pray' with their convoluted, often mystifying, categories of prayer, divided according to those new to prayer and to those described as proficients.

Weil, an intellectual of the highest order, offers a simple way of prayer, one based on the development of our power of attention:

> If we concentrate our attention on trying to solve a problem of geometry, and if at the end of an hour we are no nearer to doing so than at the beginning, we have nevertheless been making progress each minute of that hour in another more

mysterious dimension. Without our knowing or feeling it, this apparently barren effort has brought more light into the soul. The result will one day be discovered in prayer. Moreover, it may very likely be felt in some department of the intelligence in no way connected with mathematics. Perhaps he who made the unsuccessful effort will one day be able to grasp the beauty of a line of Racine more vividly on account of it. But it is certain that this effort will bear its fruit in prayer. There is no doubt whatever about that.[19]

In a day when attention deficit disorders are pandemic, her theory of attention-as-prayer astounds us. No effort of attention is ever wasted, she insists, and it prepares us for prayer! Such a marriage of seeming opposites opens the door, offering hope to many of us who feel we have failed in our efforts at prayer, we who have practiced techniques of breathing, repetition of mantras, and contorted ourselves into exotic *mudras* in order to improve our prayer-life, as well as purchasing prayer books that end up on shelves collecting dust, either unread or rejected as obscure, or too esoteric to understand and follow.

Merton, not yet a convert to Catholicism or a monk, had been for much of his young adult life unconsciously preparing himself for a life of prayer. His close, critical, examination of Fra Angelico's painting, for instance, proved he was capable of losing himself in something other, the loss of ego the necessary lever of transcendence. And his amazing insight about yoking prayer and looking (attention) as a 'sort of prayer' links him with Simone Weil whom T.S. Eliot, no less, held in awe. Eliot writes, 'We must simply expose ourselves to the personality of this woman of genius, of a kind of genius akin to that of the saints.'[20]

Merton was far from finished with Fra Angelico's painting. He then offers a moving, profound explication of theme: 'The action of the picture has no past and no future: it is full of movement and life and joy as well as utter peace and serenity: but does not *move*. It has been still for seven centuries, obviously.'[21] He proceeds to offer his thoughts on time and eternity, a philosophical commentary on the painting that equals in insight his verbal description of the painting. If the best criticism of art is the best description, then Merton measures up wonderfully, but the best criticism, I believe, also plunges into meaning, which Merton is not afraid to address.

The next painting Merton closely scrutinized was Bruegel's *The Wedding Dance*. It is one of wild celebration with people drinking, dancing, and flirting, in general having a grand time. Merton's first reaction to the painting is positive: 'The formal arrangement of the picture is very exciting and moving.'[22] He then permits a personal response: he sees these characters celebrating a wedding as unhappy people escaping their mundane lives by drunkenness and lascivious behavior. His response is, I believe, a case of psychological projection by an earthy young man manifesting an early *contemptus mundi*. He suddenly shifts his gaze to a small figure of a man at the top of the painting and writes:

> The first pyramid of dancers is carried on right into the back of the canvas by trees, people, etc., and suddenly you notice, at the apex of this pyramid, like the Keystone of the whole picture, one, rigid, solitary, little man in grey with his back to the whole business, simply looking away at nothing, off at the back and top of the picture. He is paying no attention to anything, doing nothing, just standing, ignoring everything of the subject matter, and yet being an essential element in the construction of the whole picture.[23]

Besides being an intriguing deconstruction of the painting, it is also a prophetic piece of writing. The little man in gray turns away from the wedding dance just as Merton soon turns away from the world by entering a severe, medieval-like monastery to live a life of silence and solitude, in a place where, he believes, he will begin to pray in earnest. But again, his prayer life has already been well launched; in fact, I believe that Merton's prayer life commenced when his young eyes focused on the beauty of nature, the very beauty his father attempted to capture on canvas.

Merton also appreciated El Greco; it is rather amusing to read his journal commentaries on other people's reactions to the great painter, especially their facile remarks about the artist's tubercular-like figures. Merton adds his own opinion:

> Yet so many people were articulate about the pictures, and shouted at them, anyway. And what's the difference between

the dame with the TB gag and the ones who like El Greco because he is in fashion, provisionally, before finding out? Because nowadays El Greco is not for a lot of people and perhaps he never was. That is, he is plenty complex, and most people cannot get at him all at once because they are not all that complex themselves. Anyway, El Greco has a lot of weaknesses, too, compared to Angelico for example. (Yet, do not deny anything of the power and perfect form of the Adoration of the Shepherds in the Metropolitan.) But when he fails the failures are striking. People honestly liked the Bruegel, I guess, they all had an acquired respect for Rembrandt. No boast, no false humility either.[24]

Perhaps he sounds a bit brash, if not arrogant, but one cannot help admiring the confidence of his opinions. And, again, we must remember, Merton was not studying art at Columbia. His life with his artist father, as well as his years spent with his cultured guardian Tom Bennett, served as a liberal arts education, with an emphasis on literature and the visual arts.

Another analysis of an Old Master, as Auden described such painters, shows again how Merton's attention to art was a close one, as well as astute and wisely insightful. About Hieronymus Bosch's *Adoration of Kings*, he writes:

The Hieronymus Bosch *Adoration of Kings* that was in the World's Fair, not this year but last. The surrealism of Bosch is tolerated by people (who don't like art) on the grounds that Bosch lived in the old days and didn't know any better. In other words it must have been unconscious on his part. Nobody who could draw as *real* a Christ Child as Bosch — real in the sense that it is not realistic, but the incarnation of reality — of actuality, i.e. goodness, power — could do anything unconsciously in his painting![25]

Here Merton has a secure handle on several matters: his artistic eye is focused, not in the least intimidated by Bosch, an artist whose spiritual/psychological depth can often overwhelm viewers. Merton zeros in on the Christ figure by a sacrifice of ego that becomes an act of prayerful attention. The proof of his sharp powers of attention is that he is actually remembering an act of attention: it has been a year since he viewed the painting, but its details are still freshly present. He is able to bring forth the painting onto the screen of memory as if he were again attending the World's Fair. He also has gained a firm grasp on surrealism with its roots in the unconscious. Merton was definitely a man of his time, well versed in the commerce of current ideas and theories.

As God touched Merton in Rome while he stood before the great Byzantine mosaics, he again touched him, this time through the beauty of Fra Angelico and Bruegel and Bosch.

Merton was at his critical best in his commentary on the Picasso exhibition held in New York in 1939. He exudes appreciation for the Spanish painter: 'The man is an immense and unheard of genius. They are pictures that are perfect because they are the way they are.'[26] Merton understood full well that Picasso's great talent was to see the world as it really is. This capacity to see what is in front of us − the 'isness' or what Merton's favorite poet, Gerard Manley Hopkins, calls (borrowing from Duns Scotus) the *haecceitas* of things − renders a thing miraculously unique whether it be a tree or an apple lying on a white plate.

To see well is the beginning of the spiritual life. Merton writes, 'The first step in the interior life, nowadays, is not, as some might imagine, learning not to see and taste and hear and feel things. On the contrary, what we must do is begin by unlearning our wrong ways of seeing, tasting, feeling, and so forth, and acquire a few of the right ones.'[27]

Simone Weil also had an eye for the visual arts, and when visiting Florence, she spent hours at the Uffizi Gallery, gazing a long time on her favourite painting, Giorgione's *Concert,* but her description of Leonardo da Vinci's *The Last Supper* is extraordinary. She writes:

> There is a point on the hair on the right side of Christ's head toward which all the perspective lines of the roof converge and also, approximately, the lines formed by the Apostles' hands on each side of him. But this convergence …exists only in the two-dimensional space which it evokes. Thus there is a double composition, and through a secret, subtle influence that helps to make his serenity appear supernatural, the eye is

led back from everywhere toward the face of Christ.....There's no defensible reason not to spend one's life in the refectory of this convent.[28]

Her appreciation of *The Last Supper* is similar to Merton's of Fra Angelico: both offered their complete attention to a painting and lost themselves in it, and both returned from their attention with a deeper understanding. Merton's is a more thematic one whereas Weil's is almost mathematical – not surprising since her brother, André, was a mathematical genius, and Weil maintained a lifetime interest in mathematics. Her analysis also underscores her theory of prayer: perspective lines vanish in Christ as the ego should vanish in prayer. Remember, for instance, her memorization of Herbert's poem, 'Love': by giving her complete attention to the poem, she entered a prayerful state, for the poem's subject matter is Christ's unconditional love. A similar dynamic occurs with *The Last Supper*. By offering it her complete attention, even to the point of following the perspective lines, she loses herself only to find herself gazing at the face of Christ, the result of attention: one could simply say that attention to beauty brings us to Christ, a comment I do not believe Weil would contest.

After Merton entered the Abbey of Gethsemani, he could not visit museums and galleries, and the astute sharpness of his artistic eye faded with time. When he began to write a book called *Art and Worship*, addressing sacred art, he failed to find a publisher because he had lost contact with contemporary art, and many of his ideas were dismissed as naive and uninformed. For the first fifteen years of his monastic life, his aesthetic needs were met by Gregorian chant, the Mass, *lectio divina* and the natural beauty of the location of the Abbey of Gethsemani in the hills of Kentucky. With visual art unavailable, Merton still continued to sharpen his powers of attention, but his focus was now the word, the Logos, of God. Let us now look closely at *lectio divina*.

When Merton was a boy of ten, his father encouraged him to read William Blake. Merton writes:

> Father had always liked Blake, and had tried to explain to me what was good about him when I was a child of ten. The funny thing about Blake is that although the *Songs of Innocence* look like children's poems, and almost seem to have been written for children, they are, to most children, incomprehensible. Or at least, they were so to me.[1]

Nevertheless, Blake's verse had made an impact and, as a sixteen-year-old student at Oakham, he again tackled Blake's mystical poetry. Merton writes:

> And all the time I reflected, that afternoon, upon Blake. I remembered how I concentrated and applied myself to it. It was rare that I ever really thought about such a thing of my own accord. But I was trying to establish what manner of man he was. Where did he stand? What did he believe? What did he preach? … How incapable I was of understanding anything like the ideals of a William Blake! How could I possibly realize that his rebellion for all its strange heterodoxies, was fundamentally the rebellion of the saints.[2]

For Merton to offer his complete attention to a symbolic, often enigmatic poet like Blake, and to struggle to understand him, is a testament to his precocious intellectual gifts, and the questions he attempted to answer reveal a questing teenager trying to understand not only Blake's life but his own. Consider his probing questions: 'What manner of man?' 'Where did he stand?' 'What did he believe?' 'What did he preach?' 'What were his ideals?' So many soul-searching questions, and therein lay his fascination with Blake, a rebel who questioned everything – like the young Merton himself.

A year later, back from his European trip, and recovering from an infected foot, Merton received on loan from Oakham's headmaster a volume of Gerard Manley Hopkins' poetry. Merton again tackled a rather difficult poet, famous for his obscurity, sprung rhythm, 'instress' and 'inscape.' At first, Merton was wary of Hopkins because he was a Jesuit, and Merton had not escaped the stereotypical notion some non-Catholics have about the 'secretive and wily' Jesuits. But Hopkins' mastery of imagery and language, in addition to his sacramental view of nature, captivated the fledgling poet. Furthermore, in many ways Merton and Hopkins were alike:

> Both attended English prep school and college, Hopkins at Oxford, Merton at Cambridge.
> Both were converts.
> Both were linguistically gifted.
> Both were artistic, preferring drawing to painting.
> Both were poets.
> Both kept detailed journals
> Both considered becoming Franciscans.
> Both were priests.
> Both were in conflict about writing verse and only continued writing it at the instruction of their superiors.
> Both were passionate about nature.

Merton wrote his master's thesis on Blake and had submitted a proposal to write his doctoral dissertation on Hopkins, but it was refused. Shortly after, when Merton was reading Lahey's biography of Hopkins, at the point where John Henry Newman accepts Hopkins into the church, Merton shut the book and headed to Corpus Christi Church to seek Father Ford to begin Catholic instruction. Several years later, in 1941, when Merton began to divest himself of his worldly possessions, the first step in readying himself to enter the Cistercian Abbey of Gethsemani in Kentucky, he kept only five books. Two were books of poetry: Blake and Hopkins.

On entering a monastery, Merton had in effect renounced the world. Much has been made of his *contemptus mundi*, and justifiably so because Merton had viewed the modern world as corrupt (T.S. Eliot had felt the same); in his autobiography, Merton had written that Gethsemani was the center of America, a spiritual powerhouse keeping the country from falling apart.

In renouncing the world, Merton had also given up the visual arts. He would no longer be visiting galleries or museums, an integral, enriching and exciting part of his secular life. His *Vita Nuova* offered him a new focus for his attention: Scripture. For nearly two thousand years Scripture had been the primary means of Christian formation, producing scholars, saints, mystics, theologians, philosophers, priests, nuns, missionaries, artists and poets as well as holy lay men and women. Its importance in Christian life cannot be overestimated:

> The church employs its Scriptures for the attainment of human authenticity in Christian conversion, conceived as both event and lifelong process. Its pedagogy aims at the transformation of the cognitive and affective consciousness of human subjects, of the decision-making and activity of responsible human agents, in every sphere of their relational existence (intrapersonal, interpersonal, social, national, international).[3]

As a monk, Merton's every waking hour was imbued with Scripture. During a two-week period, he would chant in choir the complete psalter. At every Mass he would read portions of the Old and New Testament. Private meditation also focused on Scripture. All such reading falls under the term *lectio divina*.

> *Lectio divina* for Saint Benedict meant careful and attentive reading of the scriptures and of other sacred writings, especially the monastic Fathers. It was done with a conscious openness of heart to the Holy Spirit, who was perceived to be speaking to the individual through the sacred text: it was thus closely linked to prayer and became a primary source of spiritual growth. *Lectio* also involved learning by heart the psalms and other passages of scripture. It was this discipline of *lectio* that gave rise, in the dark times that were to come, to

the emergence of Benedictine monasteries as centers of literacy and of learning in scripture and theology.[4]

In addition to the *Horae Canonicae*, the Rule of St Benedict envisages an additional three hours of *lectio divina*. Scripture should be read slowly, preferably in small segments, and then pondered upon. This allows for meditation. Meditation leads into a deeper form of prayer called contemplation, a form of self-forgetting prayer that is imageless. But the first step in such prayer is often a line or passage from Scripture. Cistercian Michael Casey writes, '*Lectio divina* is like reading poetry: we need to slow down, to savor what we read, and to allow the text to trigger memories and associations that reside below the threshold of awareness.'[5]

Before his entry into Gethsemani, Merton was a man of the book and a close reader of the classics as well as modern poetry and contemporary novels; of course, he also wrote poems and novels. He was also well versed in mystical literature; shortly after his baptism, he had read St Ignatius Loyola, Teresa of Avila, and St John of the Cross. For thirty days at his Perry Street apartment, he followed the Ignatian *Spiritual Exercises* with its four-fold purpose:

> The four points of the Exercise then proceed to demonstrate how God shares with humankind: first, by the gifts he gives, such as Creation itself, Redemption by Christ, and the particular gifts of one's own life; then, how God not only gives to us but even dwells in his creatures – in the elements of the earth, in plants, in animals, above all in mankind, his image; next, how God acts, even labors, with all created things, charging them as it were with the energy of their being; finally and climactically, the exercitant is asked to imagine all these gifts – filled with God's presence and energy – descending from heaven, like the rays of light from the sun or water from a fountain. Clearly the movement is into deeper and deeper union between ourselves and God, a deeper intensity of relationship.[6]

He had also read several times one of the century's most difficult texts, James Joyce's *Ulysses*, an exercise that would surely help him as a monk (the irony being that Joyce was a spoiled priest and Merton would become one).

Merton was not always a close and patient reader:

> I often wonder if teaching literature hasn't been the first thing to make me really read the stuff. I feel as if I never had read any literature before! I wonder what I have been doing with books all this time. I certainly have to wear reading glasses, so I was using my eyes. But somewhere it all got lost, didn't read carefully all that I read: and I wonder how many things I've read I can remember? I certainly can't quote![7]

He then lists what he can remember: a line or two of Dante, Shakespeare, Blake, Wordsworth, Keats, Hopkins, and a snippet of a jazz lyric: 'I'll tell you the story of Minnie the Moocher/She was a low down Hoochie Koocher'[8] But the important thing is that he had offered his attention, often acutely so, to something other. And this, according to Simone Weil, prepared him for prayer, for as a monk his chief duty is focusing his attention on *lectio divina*. As he once memorized literature and contemporary song lyrics, he would now memorize, by heart, portions of Scripture. Implicit in such activity is Plato's dictum, 'We become what we behold'; thus, the monk hopes daily to become more and more Christ-like.

As a teacher of English literature, Merton had to learn to master what the French describe as *explication de texte*. We need only listen to his tapes while teaching the novices William Faulkner's *The Bear* or Rilke's 'The panther' to know that Merton was a dynamic teacher as well as a close reader of the text. And it is this gift that Merton brings to *lectio divina*, one that nourishes his monastic life, helping him to become a devoted and committed Trappist monk.

Even when Merton considered himself a poor reader, he was indeed nourishing his soul. Weil writes, 'Perhaps he who made the unsuccessful effort (of attention) will one day be able to grasp the beauty of a line of Racine more vividly on account of it. But it is certain that this effort will bear its fruit in prayer. There is no doubt whatever about that.'[9]

So it is not surprising to realize that the central theme of *The Sign of Jonas* is books, both the reading and writing of them. Under orders from his abbot to write, Merton continues to compose poetry and to complete his books on Mother Berchmans and St John of the Cross, amongst others.

The Seven Storey Mountain (1948) becomes a runaway bestseller while he is composing *The Sign of Jonas* (1953). But Merton is ambivalent about being a famous author. He writes, 'Every book I write is a mirror of my own character and conscience. I always open the final, printed job, with a faint hope of finding myself agreeable, and I never do.'[10]

He begins to doubt himself, even to question his vocation. He had hoped to disappear into 'God alone,' but finds himself still very much a part of the world, particularly the sometimes ruthless, moneymaking publishing world. Against the Order's usual practice, he is allowed to have visitors, like the publisher James Laughlin of New Directions Press who, to Merton's initial chagrin, publishes writers like Henry Miller.

Merton also begins to fear that perhaps he does not have what it takes to become a true contemplative. He chastises himself for such doubt, 'I find myself accepting the idea that perhaps I do not have a purely contemplative vocation. I say "accept." I do not *believe* it. It is utterly impossible for me to believe any such thing: everything in me cries out for solitude and for God alone.'[11]

He is obviously a monk caught in a spiritual crisis, and the only thing he can do is to plod on and continue to pray by offering his complete attention to ritual and Scripture, in the hope of divine assistance.

There are consolations, particularly in the Mass: 'I love the prayers that go with the incensation at a solemn Mass – the prayers and the ceremonies. These too, are so easy and simple and happy!'[12] He will soon be able to celebrate Mass as a priest, hoping that the Mass may 'lighten the atmosphere and be a step forward to heaven and to vision.'[13]

The day of his ordination is clearly the high point of his life, a time of great happiness and fulfilment. He has finally become what he believes God wants him to be. He writes, 'The Mass is the most wonderful thing that has ever entered into my life. When I am at the altar I feel that I am at last the person that God has truly intended me to be.'[14]

As a priest, Merton begins to read Scripture more thoroughly, lamenting his novitiate years: 'How little Scripture I used to read in the novitiate! I remember walking in the garden on summer mornings and reading Jeremiah and also Saint Paul, but not very consistently.'[15] He now reads it closely as he had once read James Joyce, each word carefully pondered:

> Every word that comes from the mouth of God is nourishment that feeds the soul with eternal life ... By the reading of Scripture I am so renewed that all nature seems renewed around me and with me. The sky seems to be a pure, a cooler blue, the trees a deeper green, light is sharper on the outlines of the forest and the hills and the whole world is charged with the glory of God and I feel fire and music in the earth under my feet.[16]

This entry illustrates the influence of Hopkins, Merton speaking Hopkins-like language, except for the difference of one word: Merton, 'the whole world is charged with the glory of God'; Hopkins, 'The world is charged with the grandeur of God.'

Spiritual insight has cleansed his doors of perception, revealing the true beauty of nature: 'cooler blue,' 'deeper green,' and 'light is sharper.' This is what the mystic journey entails, for Merton has set himself on the mystic quest: through monastic life to be granted a glimpse of God.

Like another poet with a mystical temperament, Theodore Roethke, Merton would not be satisfied with a life lived only on the surface; and the way to this deeper life in God is through attention. Roethke writes:,

> To look at a thing so long that you are a part of it and it is a part of you — Rilke gazing at his tiger for eight hours, for instance. If you can effect this, then you are by way of getting somewhere: knowing you will break from self-involvement, from I to Otherwise or maybe to Thee.[17]

Notice the spiritual movement of the contemplative: it moves from 'I' to 'Otherwise,' and then the great possibility, always a grace, to God: 'Thee.'

In the beginning of his monastic life, Scripture had been the recipient of Merton's long look, i.e. total immersion, by attention, in *lectio divina*. There are degrees of attention:

The glance
The cursory look
The look
The long look (self-forgetting, therefore, contemplative)

Merton is obviously more concerned with the long look, the contemplative look. When Merton meditates on Scripture under the open sky, he afterwards gazes upon nature, which now appears more radiant, with a Hopkins-like deep-down freshness. He becomes aware of a higher level of reality, gifted with a sense of sublimity, like a whiff of paradise and a hint of divinity. It is what Merton needs at this stage of his spiritual development, for he is surely at the first stage of the mystical journey known as the Awakening.

Throughout *The Sign of Jonas*, however, Merton experiences a conflict concerning what is more worthy of his attention: Scripture or nature. In a rather dramatic passage, and sounding like Prospero bidding goodbye to his island, Merton writes:

> You flowers and trees, you hills and streams, you fields, flocks and wild birds, you books, you poems, and you people, I am unutterably alone in the midst of you. The irrational hunger that sometimes gets into the depths of my will, *tries to swing my deepest self away from God and direct it to your love.*[18] (my emphasis)

Merton still possesses an unhealthy dose of *contemptus mundi* within himself, revealed by a duality of vision that perceives danger (temptation) in nature and in people. Another example of duality appears in this entry:

> As soon as I get into a cell by myself I am a different person! Prayer becomes what it ought to be. Everything is very quiet. The door is closed but I have the windows open. It is warm − gray clouds fly − all night and all day the frogs sing ... How close God is in this room! The presence of people around me is always something that divides my attention between the world and God ... To have nothing to do but abandon

yourself to God and love God! Silence and solitude are the
supreme luxuries of life.[19]

He writes as if God is not present outside his room, in nature and
in people. There is a whiff of narcissism in this passage: he is too
self-absorbed, too exclusionary, deciding it best to remove himself
to a cell away from life; whereas the true Christian way is to turn
one's gaze from the self toward the world. There is no shame in
considering the lilies of the field when in fact Christ exhorts us to
do so. As for our neighbor: we are to love them as we love
ourselves. Which makes us pause to ask if Merton's negative
feelings about nature as well as people are projections of his shadow. Surely it is a problem involving Merton's emerging concept
of the True/False Self:

> My false and private self is the one who wants to exist outside
> the reach of God's will and God's love – outside of reality and
> outside of life. And such a self cannot help but be an illusion.[20]

Literary critic Dorothy Judd Hall observes that 'Modern consciousness is struggling to recover an immediacy that was lost long
before Descartes, though he is often targeted for blame in the
schism between self and world.' The cure lies in a redefinition of
'self,' as Gerard Manley Hopkins discerns in the retreat notes on
Ignatius Loyola's *Spiritual Exercises*:

> ... whatever can with truth be called a self is not a mere centre
> or point of reference for consciousness or action attributed to
> it. Part of this world of objects, this object-world, is also part of
> the very self in question. A self then will consist of a centre, a
> surrounding area or circumference, of a point of reference and
> a belonging field.'[21]

Merton's distrust of God's world and people is one he would
gradually overcome. And there is no methodology to it, except a
life of sacrifice and prayer and becoming attentive to and appreciative of the beauty around him, abiding in nature and his
brothers and sisters.

Merton is so aware of nature's beauty that *The Sign of Jonas* contains more entries of prose descriptions of the Kentucky abbey than commentaries on Scripture. Merton moves into 'reading' God in nature, adopting a Hopkins-like sacramental vision of the world so that we are not surprised to observe him more often lifting his eyes from his breviary to look at the sky, a page as illuminative as the one in the book on his lap.

Merton's natural descriptions are often the journal's best writing, nearly as poetic as his mentor Hopkins. Whether consciously or not, he emulates Hopkins' long look that penetrates to an object's inscape, what Duns Scotus calls its *haecceitas*, its 'isness'; thus, by doing so, he praises its creator: God himself.

Hopkins often felt he gave too much of his attention to nature's beauty (a baffling contradiction, for God is present in all beauty) and as a penance practiced the ancient asceticism of 'custody of the eyes.' He would deny himself the joy and pleasure of looking at landscape and skyscape, and this must have been an exacting penance for Hopkins was truly a master of the long look, if not an eye-ecstatic.

Merton suffered a similar anxiety:

> And so I live alone and chaste in the midst of the holy beauty of created things, knowing that nothing I can see or hear or touch will ever belong to me, ashamed of my absurd need to give myself away to any one of them or to all of them. The silly, hopeless passion to give myself away to any beauty eats out my heart. It is an unworthy desire, but I cannot avoid it.[22]

Simone Weil wisely understood mankind's need for beauty: 'The beautiful is a carnal attraction which keeps us at a distance and implies a renunciation. This includes the renunciation of that which is most deep-seated, the imagination. We want to eat all the other objects of desire. The beautiful is that which we desire without wishing to eat it. We desire that it should be.'[23] Another of her comments would have quieted Merton's anxiety; she writes, 'The value of a religious or, more generally, a spiritual way of life is appreciated by the amount of illumination thrown upon the things of the world.'[24]

Generally speaking, both poets would have saved themselves from much anxiety if they had had access to Weil's belief in the 'implicit love of God' that addresses 'experiences in which God is present though unrealized by the person involved in the experience. These experiences are those which are constituted by the apprehension of the beauty of the world, the love of our neighbor, and participation in the orthodox religious acts of the worshipping church … that within the love of the beauty of the world is hidden the longing for the Incarnation.'[25]

As ambivalent as he is, Merton cannot resist the beauty of Kentucky's landscape with its hills and woods blazing in red, copper and brown, its sky clear except for the occasional buzzard. Within the abbey's enclosure he prays and reads, saturating the cloistered ambience 'with my prayers and with the Psalms and with the books I read out here under the trees, looking over the wall, not at the world but at our forest, our solitude. Everything I see has become incomparably rich for me.'[26]

Notice, however, how interpenetration has occurred within the monastic enclosure for Merton's prayers have saturated the abbey's ambience, rendering them sacred. Yet duality still lingers: 'looking over the wall, not at the world but at our forest.' Is not the forest in the world?

* * * * *

As noted, *The Sign of Jonas* contains some of Merton's finest writing: its epilogue, 'Firewatch, July 4, 1952' is a prose poem of haunting beauty. But within the covers of *The Sign of Jonas* is a prose passage as lovely as any of Merton's spontaneous prayers and Wordsworthian descriptions of Kentucky's hills and sky.

It is a lengthy entry, but it deserves attention:

> The eagle attacked a tree full of starlings but before he was near them the whole cloud of them left the tree and avoided him and he came nowhere near them. Then he went away and they all alighted on the ground. They were there moving about and singing for about five minutes. Then, like lightning, it happened. I saw a scare go into the cloud of birds, and they opened their wings and began to rise off the ground and, in that split second, from behind the house and from over my roof a hawk came down like a bullet, and shot straight into the middle of the starlings just as they were getting off the ground.

They rose into the air and there was a slight scuffle on the ground as the hawk got his talons into the one bird he had nailed.[27]

This is Hemingway-like reportage, spare and clean. Merton's eye is as sharp as the hawk's attack on the starlings. His attention misses nothing of the assault: it is instantaneous and brutally honest. Merton continues:

It was a terrible and yet beautiful thing, that lightning flight, straight as an arrow, that killed the slower starling…The hawk, all alone, in the pasture, possessed his prey. He did not fly away with it like a thief. He stayed in the field like a king with the killed bird, and nothing else came near him. He took his time.[28]

As mentioned before, Merton is often Romantic in his description of nature, but here at the approaching end of his journal, a new vision emerges. Merton sees nature as it really is, Janus-faced: he now describes nature red in tooth and claw. He has yet to embark upon his close study of Zen, but here Merton exhibits a fine example of the kind of acute attention, or what the Zennist would call 'direct seeing,' that he will come to master during his hermitage years in the mid-1960s.

Merton is so caught up in looking that he disappears. Afterwards, he records what he has seen so that we are able to see with his eyes, and what we see is a 'terrible beauty.' Implicit, of course, is Merton's imitation of the hawk. He is as swift as the hawk, willing to surrender himself to the Now moment: to look. 'Like a bullet' Merton's attention nails the subjects, both starling and hawk. The hawk does what it does, and Merton does what a writer does – as well as what a contemplative does.

But we are not finished. We must look at the next paragraph, for here we find how deeply Gerard Manley Hopkins influenced Merton. Merton says:

I tried to pray, afterward. But the hawk was eating the bird. And I thought of that flight, coming down like a bullet from the sky behind me and over my roof, the sure aim with which he hit this one bird, as though he had picked it out a mile away. For a moment I envied the lords of the middle ages who had their falcons and I thought of the Arabs with their fast horses, hawking on the desert's edge, and I also understood the terrible fact that some men love war. But in the end, I think that hawk is to be studied by saints and contemplatives, because he knows his business. I wish I knew my business as well as he does his.[29]

This passage could be a gloss of Hopkins' famous sonnet 'The Windhover: To Christ our Lord.' Hopkins also watched a hawk flying in the sky. He marvelled at its beauty, bringing to his mind medieval France and dauphins riding horses and taking pleasure in falconry. Hopkins' heart is 'stirred for a bird,– the achieve of, the mastery of the thing!/Brute beauty and valour and act.'

Merton says, 'I tried to pray, afterward.' According to Simone Weil, however, Merton is praying when he watches the hawk attack the starling: 'Absolutely unmixed attention is prayer.' Being the monk he is, he must verbally sanctify what he has just seen:

I wonder if my admiration for you gives me an affinity for you, artist! I wonder if there will ever be something connatural between us, between your flight and my heart stirred in hiding, to serve Christ, as you, soldier, serve, your nature. And God's love a thousand times more terrible! Now I am going back to the attic and the shovels and the broken window and the trains in the valley and the prayer of Jesus.[30]

He almost exactly echoes Hopkins, 'my heart stirred in hiding'; Hopkins, 'My heart in hiding/Stirred for a bird.' And both men, spiritual to their core, end in Jesus: Merton places Jesus as the last word in his passage; Hopkins places Jesus at the very beginning of his poem, 'The Windhover, To Christ our Lord.' What did Merton and Hopkins see in the hawk? They saw that the 'world is charged with the grandeur of God.' Both also understood, 'To pay attention, this is our endless and proper work.'[31]

Although he immediately recognized Simone Weil's genius, admiring her social activism and her youthful, idealistic pacifism, Thomas Merton was at first baffled by her. Like so many others, he did not know how to categorize her. He writes, 'She has been called all kinds of names, both good and bad and often contradictory: Gnostic and Catholic, Jew and Albigensian, medievalist and modernist, Platonist and anarchist, rebel and saint, rationalist and mystic.'[1]

An early Merton reference to Weil occurs in *Conjectures of a Guilty Bystander* where he compares her to Zoé Oldenbourg who passionately and beautifully wrote about the Cathars. And he comments on how one cannot help loving such compassionate and loving people (Oldenbourg and Weil).[2] By the time Merton wrote *A Vow of Conversation*, his opinion of Weil had considerably deepened; he writes, 'I am finally getting to know her. I have a lot of sympathy for her, although I cannot agree with some of her attitudes and ideas.'[3] He adds, 'What does impress me in Simone Weil is her intuition of suffering and love: her insistence on being identified with the unfortunate and with the unbeliever. The realization that God's love must break the human heart.'[4] The latter is, indeed, extraordinary praise. Then comes his stunning comment, 'Without her contribution, we would be less human.'[5]

Impressed by his reading of Weil, he celebrated a Requiem Mass for her and spoke to the novices and juniors about her love of George Herbert's poem 'Love bade me welcome,' the poem that brought her to Christ. That a poem could accomplish this would not have surprised Merton; he had written, 'Christ is the inspiration of Christian poetry, and Christ is the center of the contemplative life.'[6] But what likely intrigued Merton was Weil's aesthetic experience's being more than an analogue of mystical experience, but rather, the real thing. And as for Merton's sharing

Herbert's poem with the monks under his charge, it illustrates how moved he was by the judgement of this unorthodox woman. Here is the poem Weil memorized and wrote out by hand:

Love bade me welcome

Love bade me welcome: yet my soul drew back,
Guilty of dust and sin.
But quickeyed Love, observing me grow slack
From my first entrance in,
Drew nearer to me, sweetly questioning
If I lacked anything.

A guest, I answered, worthy to be here:
Love said, thou shalt be he.
I, the unkind, ungrateful? Ah my dear,
I cannot look on thee.
Love took me by the hand, and smiling did reply,
Who made the eyes but I?

True, Lord, but I have marred them: let my shame
Go where it deserves.
And dost thou not know, says Love, who bore the blame?
My dear, then I will serve.
Thou must sit down, says Love, and taste my meat:
So I did sit and eat.

(George Herbert)

Because of Weil's love of Herbert's poem, it has over the decades become popular with Christians and non-Christians alike. Two of our best contemporary critics, Helen Vendler and Camille Paglia, have offered penetrating exegeses of the poem. Paglia writes in her recent book:

Love's response is Zen-like: to illustrate how self-entrammeled is humanity by fallible words, he uses touch and punning to circumvent everyday logic. Taking the guest's hand, Love asks, 'Who made the eyes but I?' This brilliant sally asserts that man cannot look away from God, since everything we look at — and indeed our mental faculties as well as our organs of sight —

were made by God. These 'eyes' include the 'I' of persona identity. Love is implying – and accentuating it by electric physical contact – that our boundaries of personality are illusion and that we can find blessed relief in surrendering to the limitlessness of God.[7]

Weil would surely have appreciated Paglia's interpretation, especially its emphasis on eyes and Herbert's puns on sight and attention.

During his life, Merton had experienced a number of aesthetic experiences, dutifully recording them in his journals. But he had never claimed mystical experience, as had Weil, whose experience, he admits, had possessed 'the marks of which are to all appearances quite authentic.'[8] If Merton had experienced the mystical, he would have likely remained reticent; he says:

> The inviolability of one's spiritual sanctuary, the center of one's soul depends on secrecy, the intellectual counterpart of purity of intention. If we find God in the center of our souls, and would remain there with Him, we must bring no one else in with us, on any pretext whatever, however charitable. The best way to be charitable to your neighbor is to love God in silence and solitude and isolation – unless you are ordered or obliged to perform some special external act for others.[9]

Although Merton usually writes about prayer in the abstract, he shares spontaneous prayers appearing throughout his journals. Jonathan Montaldo has masterfully mined the journals for Merton's loveliest prayers, juxtaposing them with Merton's pen and ink drawings (more on them later) in his edited *Dialogues with Silence*. He begins with Merton's most famous prayer:

> My Lord God, I have no idea where I am going. I do not see the road ahead of me. I cannot know for certain where it will end. Nor do I really know myself, and the fact that I think I am following Your will does not mean that I am actually doing so. But I believe that the desire to please you does in fact please You. And I hope I have that desire in all that I am doing. I hope that I will never do anything apart from that desire. And I know

that, if I do this, You will lead me by the right road, though I may know nothing about it. Therefore I will trust You always though I may seem to be lost and in the shadow of death I will not fear, for You are ever with me, and You will never leave me to face my perils alone.[10]

For a rare, detailed description of Merton's private prayer, we turn to a letter to Sufi scholar Abdul Aziz. Merton writes:

Now you ask about my method of meditation. Strictly speaking I have a very simple way of prayer. It is centered entirely on attention to the presence of God and His will and His love ... Yet it does not mean imagining anything or conceiving a precise image of God, for to my mind this would be a kind of idolatry. On the contrary, it is a matter of adoring Him as invisible and infinitely beyond our comprehension, and realizing Him as all ... If I am still present 'myself' this I recognize as an obstacle about which I can do nothing unless He Himself removes the obstacle.[11]

His emphasis on 'attention' echoes Simone Weil. Any ego presence as in awareness of 'myself' is an obstacle to prayer, as Simone Weil had also believed. His letter to Aziz was written on 2 January 1967 when Merton had been living full-time in his hermitage only two years, after he had read Jacques Cabaud's biography, *Simone Weil: A Fellowship of Love*.

The Polish poet Czeslaw Milosz had inspired Merton to read Simone Weil. On 21 May 1959, Merton replied to Milosz's letter, 'I am going to have to go into Simone Weil a little. My acquaintance with her is superficial.'[12] And then a year later, he confesses he is still ignorant about this important modern voice: 'I am going to have to read Simone Weil. I know she is great and what I have read about her attracts me. Her thought as I have picked up here and there from the remarks of others is congenial to me. But the books of hers that I have looked at so far have not appealed to me, perhaps because they were in English.' And in the same letter he asks Milosz to express his admiration for her daughter to Weil's mother, again promising to 'give her (S. Weil) a direct and thoughtful reading.'[13]

Milosz had long been an admirer of Weil, early on aware of her importance as a social critic as well as a compelling spiritual writer. In 'The importance of Simone Weil,' Milosz writes:

> She has instilled a new leaven into the life of believers and unbelievers by proving that one should not be deluded by existing divergences of opinion and that many a Christian is a pagan, many a pagan a Christian in his heart. Perhaps she lived exactly for that. Her intelligence, the precision of her style were nothing but a very high degree of attention given to the sufferings of mankind. And, as she says, 'Absolutely unmixed attention is prayer.'[14]

Unfortunately Merton died before Milosz's essay was published in America, but he had followed his suggestions and read Weil's work.

Let us look at a few noticeable similarities between Merton and Weil.

> Both were born in France.
> Both had one sibling.
> Both were precocious readers, and later gifted writers.
> Both were linguists, gifted in Latin and Greek.
> Both wrote poetry.
> Both felt great compassion for the world's suffering.
> Both were drawn to the beauty of the written word as well as the visual arts.
> Both loved the early Italian artists Giotto and Fra Angelico and experienced God in Italy: Weil at Assisi when visiting the chapel Santa Maria degli Angeli where St Francis prayed; Merton in Rome before mosaics of Christ.
> Both worshipped at Corpus Christi Church, New York.
> Both were cared for by Doctor Tom Bennett: as a guardian to Merton, as a doctor to Weil.

Merton did not discover the last synchronicity until he read Jacques Cabaud's biography. Merton writes:

> A curious thing! Finishing the book on Simone Weil (*Simone Weil: A Fellowship of Love*, by Jacques Cabaud), I discover that it

was Tom Bennett, my godfather and guardian, who tried to treat her in the Middlesex Hospital and had her transferred to Ashford because she refused to eat and rejected his care. Funny that she and I have this in common! We were both problems for this good man.[15]

In their appreciation of Gregorian plainchant, Merton and Weil both meet in perfect understanding, finding its spare beauty haunting and unworldly. Merton writes:

But the cold stones of the Abbey church ring with a chant that glows with living flame, with clean, profound desire. It is an austere warmth, the warmth of Gregorian chant. It is deep beyond ordinary emotion, and that is one reason why you never get tired of it.

Gregorian chant that should, by rights, be monotonous because it has absolutely none of the tricks and resources of modern music, is full of a variety infinitely rich because it is subtle and spiritual and deep, and lies rooted far beyond the shallow level of virtuosity and 'technique,' given in the abysses of the spirit, and of the human soul.[16]

In 1938, the year Merton decided to become a Catholic, Simone Weil spent Holy Week at the Benedictine Abbey of St Peter in Solesme, France, famous for its liturgical revival. She writes:

I was suffering from splitting headaches, each sound hurt me like a blow; by an extreme effort of concentration I was able to rise above this wretched flesh, to leave it to suffer by itself, heaped up in a corner, and to find a pure and perfect joy in the unimaginable beauty of the chanting and the words. This experience enabled me by analogy to get a better understanding of the possibility of loving divine love in the midst of affliction. It goes without saying that in the course of these services the thought of the Passion of Christ entered into my being once and for all.[17]

Although Merton converted to Christianity, Weil refused to be baptised. But ever since her haunting experience of Christianity while visiting Portugal, she ever afterwards considered herself a Christian. She had visited a little Portuguese village when the women inhabitants were celebrating the feast of their patron saint. When the women began to sing their ancient Catholic hymns, Weil was overwhelmed: 'I have never heard anything so poignant ... There the conviction was suddenly borne in upon me that Christianity is pre-eminently the religion of slaves, that slaves cannot help belong to it, and I among others.'[18]

She believed Christian baptism would be a betrayal to 'the immense and unfortunate multitude of unbelievers.' A cradle Catholic, Milosz accepted Weil's decision not to be baptised a Christian (rumour is that she may have been baptised before she died), but her decision did not imply a lack of love for the church. He writes:

> She strongly believed in the presence, real and not symbolic, of Christ in the Eucharist. She considered belonging to the Church a great happiness. Yet she refused herself that happiness. In her decision not to be baptised and to remain faithful to Christ but outside of His Church, we should distinguish two motives. First, her feeling of personal vocation, of obedience to God who wanted her to stay 'at the gate' all her life together with all the neo-pagans. Second, her opposition to the punitive power of the Church against the heretics.[19]

Like Thomas Merton, Weil had been a teacher. She taught young girls, and she was also a professor of philosophy at the *lycées* of Le Puy, Auxerre and Roanne (1931–34); she taught philosophy at Bourges and later at Saint-Quentin (1935–36).

Classroom teaching provided her insights about attention, a theme she beautifully writes about in her essay, 'Right use of school studies with a view to the love of God'. The true purpose of education, she contends, is to develop our powers of attention, which demand will and effort. 'Attention,' she writes, 'consists of suspending our thought, leaving it detached, empty and ready to be penetrated by the object.'[20] And the supreme object of attention is God; thus, authentic prayer is pure attentiveness directed toward God.

Weil is said to have been a poor teacher, often overwhelming her students with minutiae delivered in a monotone voice. Merton, however, was a dynamic teacher. He was the Weilian teacher *par excellence*. To discover his effectiveness as a teacher, one need only listen to a tape recording of his teaching of the monks at Gethsemani.

Listening to his tape 'Poetry and the imagination,' we hear that Merton was a superb practitioner of Weil's philosophy of attention as presented in her groundbreaking essay. He reminds his monks that the poet Rilke worked as an assistant to the sculptor Rodin, who suggested that if Rilke truly wanted to learn to see, he should take himself to the zoo and closely observe the animals. (The refrain of Rilke's autobiographical novel, *The Notebooks of Malte Laurids Brigge*, is 'I am learning to see.')

Rilke took his mentor's advice, and the fruit of his visitations is Rilke's now world-famous poem, 'The panther'. Rilke learned his lesson well: one must look until the 'I' disappears, until the observer and the observed become one in an act of pure attention. The bars of the cage that separate the see-er from the seen represent all those aspects of the ego that keep us from pure seeing. Rilke learns that to become a poet one must learn self-forgetting. Weil teaches, however, that self-forgetting leads to attention which leads to prayer. Merton agrees with her:

> The monk is trying to understand when in fact he ought to try to *look*. The apparently mysterious and cryptic sayings of Zen become much simpler when we see them in the whole context of Buddhist 'mindfulness' or awareness, which in its most elementary form consists in that 'bare attention' which simply sees what is right there and does not add any comment, any interpretation, any judgment, any conclusion. It just sees. Learning to see in this manner is the basic and fundamental exercise of Buddhist meditation.[21]

Listening to the tape, we hear Merton's leading his monks through an exegesis of Rilke's poems: 'The panther,' 'The rose window' and 'The unicorn.' He reads aloud several English translations as well as the original German. His attention is fixed on the text, evaluating translations for accuracy, ever aware that the translation never equals the original. The thrust of his teaching is for the monks to have a poetic experience by personally connecting with the poetry. He suggests that it is best at first to disregard the poet, his reputation and his place in modern verse, and to trust their feelings about the poem. Thus, by unmediated attention, they become involved in an intimate re-creation of the poem, becoming themselves artists with the potential of inner transformation.

Weil's concept of attention was certainly on Merton's mind while writing *A Vow of Conversation*. He writes:

> The voice of God is not clearly heard at every moment; and part of the 'work of the cell' is *attention*, so that one may not miss any sound of that voice. What it means, therefore, is not only attention to inner grace but to external reality and to one's self as a completely integrated part of that reality. Hence, this implies also a forgetfulness of oneself as totally apart from outer objects, standing back from outer objects; it demands an integration of one's own life in the stream of natural and human and cultural life of the moment. When we understand how little we listen, how stubborn and gross our hearts are, we realize how important this inner work is. And we see how badly prepared we are to do it.[22]

Compare the above with Weil's commentary:

> Attention is the only faculty of the soul which gives access to God. Mental gymnastics rely on an inferior, discursive form of attention, which reasons. Properly directed, however, this attention may give rise in the soul to another, of the highest kind, which is intuitive attention. Pure, intuitive attention is the only source of perfectly beautiful art, truly original and brilliant scientific discovery, of philosophy which really aspires to wisdom and of true, practical love of one's neighbors. This kind of attention when turned to God is true prayer.[23]

They both agree that access to God is by attention, that it should be our main work, that a literal monastic cell is unnecessary for we all have within us a heart's cell.

Under the title of 'The answer of Minerva: pacifism and resistance in Simone Weil,' Merton's review of Jacques Cabaud's *Simone Weil: A Fellowship of Love* appeared in two books, *Faith and Violence* and *Thomas Merton on Peace*. He devotes more time to Weil's participation in the peace movement of the 1930s than he does to her mysticism. And this is also true with Milosz. Had she been an orthodox mystic like St Francis of Assisi, St Teresa of Avila or St John of the Cross, they perhaps may have felt more comfortable writing about this aspect of her life. But the fact of the matter is that since the publication of her writings she has exerted a tremendous impact on contemporary spirituality, one that continues to grow and spread. It has resulted in many books about her, by eminent writers such as Robert Coles and Eric Springsted.

Merton's review of the first biography of Weil by Cabaud was a positive and appreciative one. And more than three decades after Merton's death, Cabaud was still pursued about Weil. Asked by an interviewer about the title of Weil's most famous book, *Waiting for God*, Cabaud says:

> For want of a better word, 'waiting' is the one used to translate the French word 'attente.' And 'attente' is more closely related to 'attention,' than is the English 'waiting.' And *'attention'* is *synonymous with 'contemplation.'* Thus does the soul that remains in its place, 'waiting; not motionless, nor shaken or displaced by any shock from without,' thus does the soul bear spiritual fruit from 'the seed of divine love thrown into' it. For we have here to guide us the analogy of what takes place when we become aware of a truth. The mind remains in the state of suspension essential to contemplation. Attention is linked to desire. It is not linked to the will, but to desire ... The very density of these formulations points out that we are entering the mystical area, that for which the soul was made when it was created by God ... It is only when we think of God that we can think with maximum of attention.[24] (My italics.)

'Attention is synonymous with contemplation.' Merton and Weil would be pleased by his comment.

ALONE WITH THE ALONE

In the first entries of Merton's journal *A Vow of Conversation*, we instantly recognize that this Cistercian monk is far from conventional, for he announces that it is the year of the dragon, celebrated by a red Japanese kite and bamboo shafts stuck into the ground of the abbey's Zen garden, where Merton and the novices had once observed the eclipse of the moon.

Reading his journal, we feel as if we are strolling through a Zen garden of Japanese emblems: raked pebbles and sand, carefully placed rocks, pruned trees and sculptured bushes, stone benches for rest and perhaps meditation on Zen art, Zen books and Zen practices. We even meet an eminent, elderly, wise Zen monk when Merton chronicles his visit to New York City to meet Dr Daisetz Suzuki, the foremost twentieth-century Zen scholar.

It is 1964, and Merton is not yet a full-time resident of his cinder-block hermitage, staying only during the daytime, but he understands it will prove to be an important locus in his life; he reflects, 'It is also true that the hermitage is there and that I should make the best use of it, not as a place of escape, but as a real place of prayer and self-renunciation.'[1] We cannot help remembering one of Merton's favorite poets, Rilke, who writes about his new home: 'My solitude is maintained by the fact that the room I live in is quite separate, in a special little house about fifty paces from the villa itself . . . and though mine could be no monk's life shut in and shut off in a cloister, I must try gradually to grow a cloister about myself and take up my stand in the world, with walls around me, but with God and the saints in me.'[2] Both seek a deeper life in solitude and silence, one within a real cloister, the other within a cloister of the heart.

In the spirit of Zen's singleness of purpose, if we had to reduce Merton's *A Vow of Conversation* to one theme, it would be 'learning to see,' i.e. to pay attention, an endeavour that is to become Merton's major preoccupation. He also keeps us abreast of his physical eye problems, the conjunctivitis plaguing him throughout 1964–65 along with the ointments to cure it; surely his comments are an oblique aside to cast light on spiritual eyesight also requiring an analgesic.

To allow oneself to look in a kenotic (self-emptying) fashion, when the observer and the observed become one in a moment of choiceless attention, is the aim of Zen, ultimately leading to *satori*, i.e. enlightenment, and often it takes years of *zazen*, meditation, while with some it can occur in an instant. It is a way of seeing that Merton masters during his hermitage years, the first two of which are recorded in *A Vow of Conversation*, radiantly filled with what Sister Thérèse Lentfoehr calls 'Zen transparencies': moments of direct seeing.

We encounter a Merton who is seeing his environment as if for the first time: 'Today, a cold gray afternoon. Much snow. Woods, bright with snow, loom out of the dark. Totally new vision of the Vineyard Knob. Dark, etched out with snow, standing in obscurity and in a kind of strange spaciousness that I had never observed before.'[3]

His description is not Western but Eastern, like a Japanese pen and ink print. It is also akin to Wallace Stevens' poem 'The snow man': Merton's 'I' fades so that his attention focuses only on what is in front of him, a 'new vision.' What he sees encompasses a 'strange spaciousness,' one not before observed. Is this new spaciousness the result of a diminishing 'I' allowing him to be more aware of the world? Or is it his greater solitude and silence, dispelling distractions?

His experience is like that of Robinson Jeffers, a poet Czeslaw Milosz encouraged Merton to read. Jeffers writes about Chinese artists, 'They loved landscape/And put man in his place. But why/ Do their rocks have no weight?'[4] Man is in place when he is the smallest figure in the painting, and rocks appear weightless when landscape is minus artistic ego, liberating it to float.

Direct seeing, one that refuses to rely on poetics for description, comes slowly to Merton. For instance, in one entry, he writes:

> Yesterday it snowed and there was sleet, wind and cold. Clear
> frozen surface on the new snow. Sleet like the manna in

Exodus, but useless, and after I had plowed my way around among the pine trees in a walk before Vespers, with snow flying into my eyes.[5]

His intellect habitually employs analogy, comparing sleet to manna; simile is a superfluity in Zen.

Merton's journal is filled with efforts at direct seeing:

> A great storm the other night. Some trees blew down in the woods near the hermitage, including one in the path on the way up. Pine cones and bits of branches are strewn all over the lawn and last night, too, there were strong winds fighting the side of the monastery building. I still hear them grumbling around outside like friendly beasts.[6]

It is a fine prose description but pathetic fallacy dominates: the winds' fighting and grumbling like beasts.

A few months later, describing a tanager, he again employs simile, 'There was a tanager singing like a drop of blood in the tall thin pine trees against the dark pine foliage and the blue sky with the light green of the new leaves on the tulip poplar.'[7] 'Like a drop of blood' is not new or original, and it nullifies the immediacy of the moment. Such 'poetic' impositions we will not find in the finest Zen writing and never in the haiku. But as we read the journal, we come upon passages where Merton has divested himself of the metaphoric, writing only what he sees. Here is a fine attempt at direct seeing:

> Birds. A titmouse was swinging and playing in the dry weeds by the monastery woodshed. A beautiful, small, trim being. A quail was whistling in the field by the hermitage in the afternoon. What a pure lovely sound. The sound of perfect innocence.[8]

The metaphoric mind is abandoned except in the final commentary when Merton declares the titmouse 'beautiful' and the quail's sound 'lovely' and of 'perfect innocence.' Each can stand, however, on its own without qualification.

His next entry is direct:

> A tiny shrew was clinging to the inside of the novitiate screen
> doors, trapped in the house! I took her up and she ran a little
> onto my sleeve and then stayed fixed, trembling. I put her
> down in the grass outside and she ran away free.[9]

Yes, she is free and so is Merton: content and confident enough
simply to narrate what he sees. As we read through his journal, we
find more and more such Zen-like sentences:

> Perfectly beautiful spring weather. Sky utterly cloudless all day.
> Birds singing all around the hermitage. Deep green grass.[10]

> Wonderful days. Bright, cool weather. Clear skies and green hills.[11]

> This morning, gray, cool peace.[12]

Merton realizes that learning to see is a process, and far from an
easy one:

> I see more and more that my understanding of myself and of
> my life has always been most inadequate. Now that I want
> more than ever to see, I realize how difficult it is.[13]

We are again reminded of Rilke's meeting and studying great
artists like Rodin and Cézanne, ardently believing that they are
see-ers *par excellence*. Rilke writes:

> I must learn a lot more from these people (painters), be
> attentive and awake and more grateful toward all my sur-
> roundings … I will have to go to Paris so as to view pictures,
> visit Rodin … the Russian journey is a sad testimony of my
> immature eyes, which do not know how to receive, how to
> grasp and release.[14]

A Vow of Conversation chronicles the maturing of Merton's spiritual
eye of attention obliquely alluded to when he comments that his
physical eye is 'slightly better but not yet healed.'[15]

Merton had been reading theologian Rudolph Bultmann who
writes that the kingdom of God is not some far off event but is

Here and Now. Bultmann calls it 'realized eschatology.' Merton writes:

> It (realized eschatology) means the transformation of life and of human relations by Christ *now* (rather than an eschatology focused on future cosmic and religious events – the Jewish poetic figures which emphasize the transcendence of the Son of Man).
>
> Realized eschatology is at the heart of a genuine Christian (incarnational) humanism ... the presence of the Holy Spirit, the call to repentance, the call to see Christ in man, the presence of the redeeming power of the Cross in the sacraments. These belong to the 'last age,' in which we now are.[16]

The kingdom of heaven with its life more abundant is present Now. By gazing through his hermitage windows (or field glasses), Merton sees paradise, a world 'charged with the grandeur of God,' to quote one of his favorite poets. He is perhaps approaching the time in his life when he will be able, as had another favorite poet, William Blake, 'To see a world in a grain of sand/And a heaven in a wild flower/Hold infinity in the palm of your hand/And eternity in an hour.' Such seeing is the hope of every professed contemplative.

His entry for 23 April 1964 is as radiant as any writing by Hopkins or Blake:

> Real spring weather. These are the precise days when everything changes. All the trees are just beginning to be in leaf and the first green freshness of a new smell is all over the hills. Irreplaceable purity of these few days chosen by God as His sign.
>
> I live in a mixture of heavenliness and anguish. Sometimes I suddenly see 'heavenliness.' For instance, in the pure, pure white of the mature dogwood blossoms against the dark evergreens in the cloudy garden. 'Heavenliness' too of the song of the unknown bird that is perhaps here for only one or two days, passing through. A lovely deep song. Pure, no pathos, no statement, no desire, just pure heavenly sound. I am seized by this heavenliness as if I were a child, a child mind I

have never done anything to deserve, and which is my own part in the heavenly spring. This is not of this world nor is it of my own making. It is born partly of physical anguish, which is really not deep, though. The anguish goes so quickly. I have a sense that this underlying heavenliness is the real nature of things. Not their nature, but the deeper truth that they are a gift of love and of freedom, and that *this* is their true reality.[17]

What immediately comes to mind is Christ's dictum, ' "Let the children come to me; do not prevent them, for the kingdom of God belongs to such as these." ' Merton's 'child mind' is a grace, permitting him to see and to hear the 'heavenliness' about him, particularly exhibited by the beauty of the monastic enclosure. We think not of, ' "The kingdom of God is within you" '[18] but rather of, ' "The kingdom of God is among you". '[19] The latter translation underscores what Merton encounters as a hermit: the kingdom of God, Now within and without him.

'Heavenliness' arrives when Merton sees beauty (dogwood blossoms) and hears beauty (song of the unknown bird). But it is not a case of beauty merely appearing or a matter of Horace's *carpe diem* dictum, because Merton uses a passive verb: 'I *am seized* by this 'heavenliness' as if I were a child.' Merton struggles for elucidation but concludes saying, 'I have a sense that this underlying heavenliness is the real nature of things.' Notice, 'I have a sense.' A vague statement to say the least, but it echoes Wordsworth, 'a sense sublime/Of something far more deeply interfused/Whose dwelling is the light of setting suns' – a declaration of the strength and power of belief in the unseen.

For comparison, let us look at Bede Griffiths' similar experience:

I came then to where the sun was setting over the playing fields. A lark rose suddenly from the ground beside the tree where I was standing and poured out its song above my head … Everything then grew still as the sunset faded and the veil of dusk began to cover the earth. I remember now the feeling of awe which came over me. I felt inclined to kneel on the ground … and I hardly dared to look on the face of the sky, because it seemed as though it was but a veil before the face of God.[20]

Both men were graced with a glimpse beyond the veil. Griffiths received it at the beginning of his search for meaning when he had no interest in formal religion, and Merton received it when he chose a hermit's life of deeper silence and solitude, a mature man not requiring proof of God's existence.

Merton's powers of attention are becoming exquisite: as precise as spring's 'precise days.' By precise he means that everything changes with an exactness of form and temporality, and if one is attentive, one can actually glimpse how and when trees begin 'to be in leaf.' Notice he does not merely say that the trees are leafing but, to use Hopkins' term borrowed from Duns Scotus, he describes their being, their *haecceitas*, their unique '*isness*': *to be*.

Aware of 'heavenliness,' Merton is Adam, opening his eyes for the first time. He sees white blossoms against the darkness of the evergreens: in a marriage of opposites he sees the radiance. Another physical sense is also gifted with beauty: the song of an unknown bird. Unlike Keats' nightingale or Shelley's skylark or Hardy's thrush or even Griffiths' lark, Merton cannot name his bird; he is like a pre-lingual Adam innocently listening to its beautiful song.

There is the extraordinary statement, 'Pure, no pathos, no statement, no desire, just pure heavenly sound.'[21] Here metaphoric language is superfluous, if not useless; the romantic lie of pathetic fallacy is rejected. For a poet like Merton, it is a remarkable breakthrough: he abides in the Now without thought, without emotion, without ego: HE IS.

We again think of Wallace Stevens' 'The snow man' where Stevens, too, enters a state of being that sees what is there and the nothing that is. Merton also possesses a mind of winter, stripped and 'lost' in an act of attention, a mind minus intellection, a 'child mind' of bare attention, aware of only what is there: a spring day of heavenliness.

His new vision has expanded, but paradoxically it narrows with a Zen singleness of purpose, casting new light on his vocation. He writes:

> There is no question for me that my one job as a monk is to
> live this hermit life in simple contact with nature, primitively,
> quietly, doing some writing, maintaining such contacts as are
> willed by God and bearing witness to the value and goodness
> of simple things and ways, loving God in all of it.[22]

Before 1964 ends, Merton is enamored of hermit life. He is the
self-sufficient Zen monk, cooking his own supper, so much rice
that it requires half an hour to eat, then topping it with tea. He
washes his utensils with Zen-like focus: the bowl, the pot, the cup,
the knife, the spoon, each item gleaming in a Jakob Boehme-like
luminosity. No doubt about it, Merton is happy. And his 'new
vision' comes naturally (asceticism, solitude, silence, attention),
unlike Aldous Huxley, who 'achieves' such 'vision' artificially
under mescalin. After gazing at a rose, magenta and carnation
arranged in a vase, Huxley writes:

> I was not looking now at an unusual flower arrangement. I was
> seeing what Adam had seen on the morning of his creation –
> the miracle, moment by moment, of naked existence ...
> *Istigkeit* – wasn't that the word Meister Eckhart liked to use?
> 'Is-ness.'[23]

Merton questioned Huxley about such 'mysticism.' Was it the real
thing? In 1958, he had written to Huxley about an article the
English writer had published in the *Saturday Evening Post*, 'Drugs
that shape men's minds.' Merton writes:

> It seems to me that a fully mystical experience has in its very
> essence some note of a direct spiritual contact of two liberties,
> a kind of a flash or spark which ignites an intuition ... some-
> thing more of which I can only describe as 'personal', in which
> God is known not as an object ... but as I AM, or simply AM.[24]

Merton had just been reading Vladimir Lossky's *The Vision of God*,
particularly thrilled by its declaration on ecumenism, especially the
part on oriental theology. It also has him thinking about which is
more important: contemplation or eschatology? He writes:

My faith is an eschatological faith, not merely a means of penetrating the mystery of the Divine Presence, and dwelling in Him or serving Him here and now. Yet, because my faith is eschatological, it is also contemplative, for I am even here and now in the established kingdom. I can even now 'see' something of the glory of that kingdom and praise Him who is King. I would be foolish then if I lived blindly, putting all seeing off until some imagined fulfillment, for my present seeing is the beginning of a real and unimaginable fulfillment.[25]

This is Merton's Zen 'Yea!' to God's kingdom on earth, to be seen and gloried in Now. And the Tao ('the way') of glorifying God's kingdom is to pay attention to it. So when Merton describes the deer he sees in the moonlight, he has 'sanctified his senses by looking with purity on all things', therefore becoming like God. Merton concludes, 'This is, I think, what the Zen masters tried to do.'[26]

As 1964 ends, Merton has no illusions: he understands 'solitude is not something to play with from time to time. It is going to be difficult to remain divided next year between living part-time in his hermitage and in the community; two tempos and two ways of life.'[27] He is definitely committed to his hermit way of life, for it has already gifted him with 'new vision.' But he is eager to renounce being a split personality: he wants to be a hermit. Or as he would say, he needs to be a hermit.

★ ★ ★ ★ ★

The first page of his journal entry in 1965 also begins with Zen. Merton had received a letter from John Wu, who at the time was writing his book, *The Golden Age of Zen*, and whose introduction Merton would write. Merton is not only reading about Zen; he reads theology, philosophy, poetry and even novels (Graham Greene, Albert Camus, Walker Percy, to name a few), and there was always his prodigious correspondence. But the beauty of nature competes for his attention. Again he sees deer, 'In the evening light they (deer) were hard to descry against the tall brown grass, but I could pick out at least five.'[28]

Unlike the poet Rilke, Merton did not have to visit a zoo to watch animals. Wild animals roamed near his hermitage, not imprisoned behind the bars of a cage, like Rilke's 'The panther,' a favourite poem for Merton perhaps because he had sometimes felt like a 'prisoner' while living in the monastery. He has now attained the freedom he had always longed for even back in 1949 when he dreamed of becoming a Carthusian.

He is free to practice attention. Continuing to observe deer, he is further gifted, 'A lovely moment that stretched into ten minutes or more ... When they walked they seemed to multiply, so that in the end I thought there must be at least ten of them.'[29] Abundant life doubles. It was a magical moment when the deer and Merton stare at one another. If he had been gazing at a beautiful Russian icon, like the one in his hermitage chapel, it could not have been holier than this timeless moment with the deer: a moment of true, contemplative prayer.

Literary critic George Kilcourse has addressed at length the significance of deer in both Merton's prose and poetry, especially the verse he categorized as 'poetry of the forest.' It is also useful simply to consider his sighting of deer as a sign (to use Rilke's phrase) of Merton's eyes *maturing*, a kind of seeing that the Hindus describe as *darsan*.

> *Darsan* means 'seeing' but is also sometimes translated as 'auspicious sight,' and it specifically refers to both seeing and being seen by the divine presence ... *Darsan* is revelatory, illuminating the unseen, the absolute, through the act of seeing the tangible physical world – the places of pilgrimage, the temple images, the peaks of the Himalayas, the river Ganga, the gaze of holy persons, one's guru, the saints, the renunciates. *Darsan* implies being gifted by the thing seen in a moment when the observer is receptive and respectful, and thus able truly to see.[30]

Such a sea change in the quality of attention is not unusual among spiritual men and women. J. Neville Ward writes:

> In certain moments of tranquility and happiness in the infinitely diverse experience of human love, the mind seems not to be doing anything at all; it is certainly not pursuing a series of verbal thoughts, it is simply attending in quietness and joy to

what is in front of it. *It is this faculty of the mind to attend, without one thought giving way to another, simply to be held, that is characteristic of contemplation.* Practically everyone is familiar with it. It is the commonest, wisest, safest way to God.[31] (My italics.)

Zen refers to this state of being as No Mind. Merton had been intensely reading about Zen, including John Wu's chapters of his history of Zen, as well as Suzuki's *The Zen Doctrine of No Mind*, Suzuki writes:

When thus the seeing of self-nature has no reference to a specific state of consciousness, which can be logically or relatively defined as something, the Zen masters designate it in negative terms and call it 'no-thought' or 'no-mind' . . . As it is 'no-thought' or 'no-mind', the seeing is really the seeing.[32]

As a hermit, Merton has evolved from a monk dominated by the inward gaze focused primarily on the inner life to a more spacious outward gaze, a change of perspective like a U-turn, necessary to avoid the dead-end of narcissism, the trap of which all contemplatives must ever be cautious, underscoring Christ's dictum, ' "Whoever finds his life will lose it, and whoever loses his life for my sake will find it." '

Much of the winter of 1965 is spent reading a biography of Simone Weil, as well as writing a review of it. He also records more trouble with his eye, which 'gets better only slowly.' The same with the art of attention: it improves slowly. Another entry informs us his eye is 'slightly better but not yet healed.' Nevertheless, he sees a place where the deer had slept, and he delights in knowing that they are his nearest dormitory neighbors. He also sees more clearly what his purpose in life is:

The great joy of the solitary life is not found simply in quiet in the beauty and peace of nature or in the song of birds or even in the peace of one's own heart. It resides in the awakening and the attuning of the inmost heart to the voice of God – to the inexplicable, quiet definite inner certitude of one's call to obey Him, to hear Him, to worship Him here, now today in silence and alone. In the realization that this is the whole reason of one's existence.[33]

How is one to become so awake and so attuned that one can hear the still, small voice of God? Merton has discovered the answer, 'The voice of God is not clearly heard at every moment; and part of the "work of the cell" is *attention.*' Sounding more like Simone Weil, he writes, 'I see more and more that my understanding of myself and my life has always been most inadequate. Now I want more than ever to *see.*'[34]

He possesses greater self-knowledge, a grace granted while living in his new hermitage – or to use again Rilke's phrase, in the cloister of the heart. His greater solitude is surely an aid toward self-knowledge. He writes, 'It seems to me that solitude rips off all masks and all disguises. It tolerates no lies. Everything but straight and direct affirmation or silence is mocked and judged by the silence of the forest.'[35]

We now come to Merton's last entry, perhaps one of the most beautiful in all of Merton's opus, the equal of several of his prose masterpieces, like the 'Firewatch,' 'The day of the stranger' and the 'Rain and the rhinoceros.' The entry for 6 September 1965 begins with two simple sentences:

Magenta mist outside the windows. A cock crows over at Boone's farm.[36]

If you arrange it as a haiku, it contains the needed seventeen syllables:

Magenta mist outside the windows.
A cock crows over at
Boone's farm.

This perfection of direct seeing minus poetic figures of speech is followed by a stunning prose description:

Last, evening, when the moon was rising, I saw the warm burning soft red of a doe in the field. It was still light enough, so I got the field glasses and watched her. Presently a stag came out of the woods and then I saw a second doe and then, briefly, a second stag. They were not afraid. They looked at me from time to time. I watched their beautiful running, their grazing. Every movement was completely lovely, but there is a kind of gaucheness about them sometimes that makes them even lovelier, like adolescent girls.

The thing that struck me most – when you look at them directly and in movement, you see what the primitive cave painters saw. Something you never see in a photograph. It is most awe-inspiring. The *muntu* or the 'spirit' is shown in the running of the deer. The 'deerness' that sums up everything and is sacred and marvelous.[37]

This is the kind of pure attention Merton had aspired to: Zen's direct seeing. Merton is lost in prayer; he is not a conventional monk on his knees or lost in reading a gilt-edged breviary but a man so attentive to beauty, *he* has disappeared. And as St Augustine and Simone Weil remind us, God is the source of all beauty so that when the 'snare' of beauty captures Merton's eye, he is captured (enraptured?) by God. Eckhart understands the dynamic, 'The eye with which we see God is the same eye with which He sees us.'

When Merton refers to the cave painters, he echoes Huxley's comment about seeing, under mescalin, like Adam. An echo but quite a different kind of echo – how like Merton to identify with painters, for in this stage of his life he will pick up the brush and follow in his father Owen's footsteps, not to paint representational but abstract art. Perhaps Merton is at the stage in life, to use T.S. Eliot's phrase, when hints and guesses are better caught by the austerity and sparseness of brush and ebony ink: Zen calligraphy.

THE ABSTRACT CALLIGRAPHIST

Attention flowered during the hermitage years, a process involving the emergence of Merton's artistic impulses. For two decades he had virtually no contact with the visual art world except for a few letters of correspondence with his Columbia friend, the painter Ad Reinhardt. As a monk of the Abbey of Gethsemani, he appreciated Cistercian architecture as an expression of the Order's rule and way of life, and he had enjoyed poring over large albums with pictures of European monasteries.

There was not much good art within the abbey; in fact, he cringed at the sight of plaster statues of Mary and the saints. And he deplored the holy pictures, pious depictions that Catholics used to mark the pages of their missals. He was once overjoyed that a young Swiss abbot visiting Gethsemani also shared his distaste for poor, contemporary ecclesiastical art.

By the early 1960s he was so starved for art that he picked up ink and brush and began creating his calligraphies. In 1963, he facetiously (and seriously) writes to Reinhardt:

> I am again your friendly old calligrapher, always small calligraphies down here. I am the grandfather of the small calligraphy because I don't have a big brush and because I no longer run about the temple barefoot in the frosts. But I am amiable and the smaller they get the more mysterious they are, though, in fact it is the irony of art when a calligrapher gets stuck with a whole pile of papers the same size and texture: why don't friends from New York who received all kinds of expensive samples of paper send me samples of exotic and costly materials? I invite you to pretend you are about to print a most exotic book and get samples of papers from distant Cathay and all over and then send them to your dusty old correspondent who is very poor.[1]

In 1964, during the writing of *A Vow of Conversation*, Merton falls into an 'orgy' of calligraphy-making. He sent a few to Reinhardt, who finally sent Merton some fine drawing paper. Merton records:

> Ad Reinhardt has sent all kinds of fine paper, especially some thin – almost transparent – Japanese sheets on which I have found a way of crudely printing abstract calligraphies which in some cases turn out exciting, at least to me.[2]

Why at this time does he begin calligraphy? Roger Lipsey suggests it 'arose from the surplus in him – a surplus of energy and intelligence, inquiry and camaraderie.'[3] Or is it something deeper? A 1964 journal entry offers a clue. He writes: 'One thing is certain. I am surfeited with words and typescript and print. Surfeited to the point of utter nausea. Surfeited about all with letters. This is so bad that it amounts to a sickness.'[4]

Over the years, Merton had written scores of books, journals, essays and poems. He had been pigeon-holed as America's Catholic writer (along with Fulton Sheen), inundated with requests for articles, reviews, essays, endorsements, as well as prefaces and introductions for a number of books (including John Wu, for whose book Merton composed a masterful commentary on Zen). His lament echoes Samuel Beckett's character Molloy:

> Not to want to say, not to know what you want to say, not to be able to say what you think you want to say, and never to stop saying, or hardly ever, that is the thing to keep in mind, even in the heat of composition.[5]

Although he had mastered the written word, he needed a new, revitalizing way to express himself, a way to be free of censors, abbots, critics, pundits, and even his average Catholic reader always on the look-out for a theological misstep. And Zen had offered him a perfect escape: calligraphy.

By the mid-1960s, Merton had become one of America's leading authorities on Zen (along with Alan Watts), and became fascinated with Zen calligraphy (as had Watts). Taking up calligraphy was congruent with monastic simplicity: Merton did not need a studio or expensive supplies. All he needed was himself, a brush, ink, and paper as white as his Cistercian habit.

Zennists often contend that words are useless to convey Zen; yet, paradoxically, they depend on words to teach and to preserve its tradition. However, words are not taken as direct truth, but rather as a way of conveying meaning through experience. Thus, a Zen calligrapher points towards truth through his art while at the same time expressing himself through line, form, energy, and movement – gestural actions emanating from deep within the 'Zen mind.'

Merton, of course, practiced calligraphy in his own unique fashion. He had not intended to write Japanese or Chinese language (though he made attempts to learn both) or paint traditional oriental scenes like temples, rivers, mountains, cranes and chrysanthemums. Even though he was gifted at drawing, he adopted abstract art as his medium of expression. He dipped his brush in ink and in swift, spontaneous brushstrokes he created an image, one not formed beforehand in his mind. While drawing, Merton seemingly entered a Zen No Mind, permitting his hand to draw whatever it wanted to, and the results, by Merton's admission and corroborated by others, were often extraordinary. Merton relished creating his abstract calligraphies because he need not prove or defend anything; furthermore, he was also free from having to look over his shoulder for abbatial approval. He could discard the persona of the Catholic apologist and simply be himself, a person stripped of masks, something he had long advised his readers to do.

To enter the world of abstract calligraphies is to enter *terra incognita*: he never knew what he would compose, and the images represented a part of himself he had not known or met. Images arising from his unconscious were 'once only' manifestations, to borrow Rilke's phrase, never to be repeated again. And Merton was fascinated by these gifts from his own inner depths, and he was also wise enough not to try to nail them down with interpretation, allowing the viewer to see unencumbered. This is the way he advised everyone to approach art: to pay attention and to connect on a personal level.

He was not in the dark about the Abstract Art movement in America. He alluded to Jackson Pollock in a journal entry: 'A wonderful sky all day, beginning with the abstract expressionist

Jackson Pollock dawn. Scores of streaks and tiny blue-gray clouds flung like blotches all over it.'[6] Four days after this entry, he is creating calligraphies. He writes:

> This afternoon I worked on abstract calligraphic drawings. Perhaps I did too many. Some of them are fairly good. I took a batch into the Frame House last Thursday with Ulfert Wilke and he was a big help in showing how they should be framed … I have not done much writing except letters for the last two weeks.[7]

Calligraphy served as a rejuvenating respite from writing, and for two weeks he only wrote replies to letters, a typical Merton gesture; he would not hurt the feelings of a correspondent by not answering a letter.

And obedient to his altruistic streak to share his art, he readied his calligraphies to be framed for an exhibit. This is proof that he felt confident about his work, and self-assured enough to ask the counsel of Ulfert Wilke, a member of the art department of the University of Louisville and also a friend of Merton's Columbia friend Ad Reinhardt. Wilke sought out Merton at Reinhardt's suggestion. He was exactly the friend Merton needed because Wilke was an expert calligrapher, having studied in Europe and Kyoto. Like Reinhardt, Wilke was generous in supplying Merton with fine paper as well as good advice about artistic matters such as framing and what an exhibit tour would entail.

If anyone had asked Merton why he painted, he would have very likely shrugged his shoulders and said:

> Whether an artwork is a failure or a success is, in the end, of secondary importance … If I have learned to see a little bit better, then I will definitely have gained something and the world around us will be richer … for I have come to know the world as something that surpasses me so much that I can't even make the attempt to approach it.[8]

Merton's calligraphy is a way to pay attention: by turning inward he allows his unknown self to speak to him, and because Merton chose to be reticent about his intimate spiritual life, we can only speculate about what he learned from his calligraphies. One thing is certain, his abstracts did not intimidate him, or he would not have been willing to share them. And he immediately perceives their beauty and altruistically shares it. Following Christ's counsels, 'Consider the lilies of the field,'[9] Merton allows us to consider his secret 'signs.'

When the unconscious mind needs to teach us important truths about ourselves, it employs dreams as a means of communication. And Merton has recorded several important anima dreams in *A Vow of Conversation*, the common theme being the integration of the feminine archetype. Calligraphy works in a similar manner, for surely Merton's calligraphies are letters from the inner self, obliquely pointing toward a greater psychic integration.

The primary inspirations for his abstract painting are Zen and Paul Klee. Merton writes, 'I have an obligation to Paul Klee which goes deeper, even into the order of theology. An obligation about which I have done nothing.'[10] And just before his visit to New York to meet Suzuki, he dreams about Klee:

> Last night I dreamed I had found a cool clean convent of nuns on West 114th Street near where I used to have my rooms. I seem to think less about Suzuki than about a million trifles. Will I get to the Guggenheim Museum? Will I find all the Klees in the Guggenheim Museum? Will I find Rajput paintings and Zen drawings at the Metropolitan?[11] (There were no works of Klee hanging at the time.)

How exactly Klee had influenced Merton is unclear. But Merton's description of his own calligraphies sheds light on it:

> Ciphers, signs without prearrangement, figures of reconciliation, notes of harmony, inventions perhaps, but not in the sense of 'findings' arrived at by the contrived agreement of idea and execution. Neither rustic nor urbane, primitive nor modern, though they might suggest cave art, maybe Zen calligraphy.[12]

The word 'signs' is the clue we need to understand the relationship between Klee and Merton. In Rainer Crone and Joseph Leo Koerner's book, *Paul Klee: Legends of the Sign*, we read:

> The art of Paul Klee constantly turns to three great themes: The World, the Book, the Image. It is a lifelong meditation on writing as the flesh of the world, on script as the carrier of secrets, on painting as an art of signs. At the same time Klee's work with these themes remains extremely subtle, enigmatic, and difficult to picture in words.[13]

The above could also describe Merton's work. Here is Merton's description:

> These abstractions – one might almost call them graffiti rather than calligraphies — are simple signs and ciphers of energy, acts of movement intended to be propitious. Their 'meaning' is not to be sought on the level of convention or of concept. These are not conventional signs as are words, numbers, hieroglyphs, or symbols. They could not be assigned a reference by advance agreement because it has been their nature to appear on paper without previous agreement ... However, the seeing of them may open a way to obscure reconciliations and agreements that are not arbitrary — or even to new, intimate histories.[14]

Again, the purpose is attention: to see better.

When Merton is allowed out of his abbey to visit Suzuki in New York City, he immediately heads for the Guggenheim, proof that he has not lost his love of the visual arts, so long denied nourishment during his years as a monk. There he visits a Van Gogh exhibit, 'And the Van Goghs, wheels of fire, cosmic, rich, full-bodied honest victories over desperation, permanent victory, especially in the last light-and-shadow calligraphic impasto.'[15] His eye is as sharp as ever; however, it is interesting to note that Merton is attracted not so much to Van Gogh's colours as he is to the 'night and shadow calligraphic impasto.' Van Gogh became famous for his impasto, thickly applying paint upon a canvas with a palette knife, creating a richly textured effect, the opposite of traditional smooth surfaces – in effect composing in a painterly language. And influenced by Japanese prints, Van Gogh would often outline his objects in black.

Both Merton and Van Gogh were attracted to Zen art. One of Van Gogh's famous self-portraits shows him with head shaved, posing like a Zen monk. The artist also possessed an ascetic streak, but the beauty of the world won out: he could never practice custody of the eyes with so much beauty around him.

Merton's aesthetic sensibility is similar to Van Gogh's. He writes:

> If I had never seen a Japanese print, I would probably have experienced this in a purely Western way. The sun as one thing among many, a multitude of trees, enclosure wall in foreground. But Sumiye makes this whole view *one*. One – a unity seen because the sun is in the center, a unity which is more than the total of a number of parts.[16]

Merton was delighted to have his work exhibited at Catherine Spaulding College. He writes, 'I went to Catherine Spalding College with twenty-six abstract drawings of mine that are to be exhibited there in November. They are well framed, thanks to Ulfert Wilke's advice. They look pretty good, at least to me ... Wilke says, "they are real."'[17]

Wilke's remark is indeed high praise, and for Merton it must have been like rain to parched soil. But there was one obstacle to Merton's full enjoyment of his moment of artistic appreciation: how his dear friend Victor Hammer (an artist, printmaker, hand-press printer, type designer) would respond to Merton's work. Hammer was a representational artist who had no use for abstract art, considering it a sin against the Holy Ghost.

Merton writes:

> One thing saddens and embarrasses me. Victor will be shocked at my exhibition of drawings or calligraphies or whatever you want to call them. There is no way to explain this to him, and in a way, I am on his side on principle. And they do have a meaning and there is a reason for them. An unreason reason, perhaps. I feel like writing to him and saying: 'If you heard I had taken a mistress, you would be sad but you

would understand. These drawings are perhaps worse than that, but regard them as a human folly. Allow me, like everyone else, at least one abominable vice.'[18]

What is truly sad about this entry is that Merton permits the opinion of another to dim his shining moment as a calligrapher. But on the other hand he loved Hammer like a father and wanted to please him.

However, the process of individuation demands integration: Merton could not ignore the artist in him, having a right (obligation) to allow his artistic self to come forth. To repress this aspect of his personality would be tantamount to self-inflicted wounding, if not a murdering of Merton's inner artist. Merton fortunately transcends his anxiety about Hammer (Freud's theory that fathers and sons must separate) by continuing to create more calligraphies. He writes, 'This afternoon I made myself a cup of coffee strong enough to blow the roof off the hermitage and then as a result got into an orgy of abstract drawing. Most of the drawings were awful, some of them disturbing, so that now I see that I cannot afford to play with this either in solitude.'[19]

This entry is illustrative of how Merton's calligraphy teaches him about himself. He does not reveal why some of it is 'disturbing.' But because he was an introspective man devoted to the ideal that 'an unexamined life is not worth living,' we can be sure that Merton analysed these signs from his unconscious, thereby increasing his self-knowledge.

Let us return briefly to the matter of Merton's anima integration. It is prophetic to note in Merton's journal entry on Hammer this particular sentence: 'If you heard I had taken a mistress, you would be sad but you would understand.' Merton would soon fall in love with a nurse, a torrid affair that lasts six months. Many people find this problematic, but viewing it from a psychological perspective, particularly a Jungian one, Merton is finally, by falling in love, healing himself of what he calls his 'refusal of women.' And understanding this, we can indeed follow Merton's request: allow me to be human.

Merton had the opportunity to leave the abbey to attend his exhibit. He was pleased: 'I was able to see the drawings as they are now hung at Catherine Spaulding. A very attractive exhibit.'[20]

And this exhibit embarked on a three-year tour: New Orleans, Milwaukee, St Louis, Santa Barbara, New York City and finally Washington, DC.

Merton's art is an expression of the kind of person he had become. It is also an expression of the kind of person he hopes to become. His calligraphy is simple, the result of maximum effort to create something minimalist. It is antithetical to his usual art, i.e. books and poetry. It is something of the moment, non-intellectual and purely simple. There is no self-consciousness in calligraphy: it is an outlet as well as an antidote he desperately needs to counter his self-absorbedness as a memoirist.

Calligraphy allows Merton to feel, rather than think. It allows a disappearance of ego in the exquisite moment of attentive creation: he is involved in what some would simply describe as 'fun.' Like a child, he can be unmindful while at the same time be simple and direct in order to offer his undivided attention to calligraphic gestures.

During and after the moment of creation, Merton the artist is permitted to look at his abstracts without justifying what is before him. He has no need to twist himself into some dogmatic formula. He lives in the moment without a need to transfer memory onto paper; thus, every moment is original, every abstract calligraphy one of a kind.

Calligraphy was food for the soul: it was another kind of prayer. Now we shall explore Merton's other artistic endeavor: photography.

THE CAMERA AND THE
CONTEMPLATIVE EYE

We cannot ignore Merton's other pursuit of visual art during his hermitage years: photography. His interest in photography is emblematic of his life as a contemplative, for to become a contemplative one must develop the spiritual eye of attention, and what in modern life symbolizes more fully and exactly what the life of a contemplative life entails than the camera. The camera zeroes in on the object chosen by the eye to be seen, not a cursory but a deep seeing, as if one is attempting to see into the life of things, like monks with eyes fixed upon religious ritual or Scripture, hoping for a divine glimpse. Merton diligently worked on his photography, fully appreciating it as art, and he felt blessed to have as his mentor John Howard Griffin, a master photographer.

This change of heart about photography is an interesting development in Merton's artistic growth. He once wrote, 'In any case, nothing resembles reality less than the photograph.'[1] But photography, like calligraphy, is a new reality (Pound's 'Make it new'.) Later, he qualified his earlier statement:

> Nothing resembles substance less than its shadow. To convey the meaning of something substantial you have to use not a shadow but a sign, not the imitation but the image. The image is a new and different reality, and of course it does not convey an impression of some object, but the mind of the subject and that is something else again.[2]

John Howard Griffin was famous in his own right. He wrote the bestseller *Black Like Me*, as well as one of the best novels about monastic life ever written, *The Devil Rides Outside*. He was also a medievalist and an expert on Gregorian chant. When Merton sent him his photographs, Griffin immediately perceived Merton's talent; he said, 'From my point of view, he showed great gifts,'[3] but he lamented Merton's poor camera equipment. So he loaned Merton a fine camera and lenses, knowing full well that they would be a permanent gift to his friend, presented without qualms because he had relished the joy Merton exhibited while taking pictures. By the time Griffin made his last visit to his friend, shortly before Merton's trip to Bangkok, he could confidently say about Merton, 'He had now developed a photographer's eye.'[4]

One of the perennially wise quotes to have influenced Merton's life is William Blake's 'Everything that is/Is holy.' What Merton chose to photograph is proof that nothing was unworthy of his eye, for no matter how small or hidden a thing, it is holy and by our bestowing our attention upon it, we are sanctified.

Browsing through John Howard Griffin's *A Hidden Wholeness: The Visual World of Thomas Merton*, showcasing some of the best of the monk's photographs, we see visible proof that Merton had, indeed, become a master of attention. He photographed a variety of beautiful things: emerging crocuses juxtaposed against an ancient wheel, Jackson Pollock-like pots streaked in dripping paint, skyscapes, tree roots, grass growing between rocks, ancient sawed trees revealing their secret rings of growth, an abbey post office wall its paint chipped and peeling looking like a modernist painting, and ordinary chairs and farm utensils standing solitarily numinous in a Shaker-like simplicity.

There are two extraordinary snow scenes. One is an austere shot of a few weeds sticking up through the snow beneath which is either a person's or animal's footprint, but its nearly total emptiness is stunning, suggesting not only absence but presence, so very much a monastic reality. With his 'mind of winter,' Merton is able to see 'Nothing that is not there and the nothing that is.'[5] The other snow scene is similar, a landscape depicting gnarled tree roots draped in snow. Viewing such photos, we cannot help thinking of monastic (Zen) simplicity and austerity; thus, they are emblematic of Merton's life of asceticism – the simple, unadorned monk wearing his white habit, seeking divine hints and guesses not only in religious ritual and Scripture but also in the beauty of God's world.

According to Griffin, Merton was always on the look-out for striking, unusual images to photograph, ones which most of us fail to see. Like William Carlos Williams (who shared Merton's publisher, New Directions Press), he profoundly understood that so much depends on a wheelbarrow glazed with rain and standing next to the white chickens. So much depends on everything in God's world, for like Rilke, Merton understood how transitory life is, and for much of the world's beauty, we have only one chance to look (Rilke believed that to attend to beauty is our *raison d'être*). Thus, Merton's photographs serve as covert homilies: 'Look now, for you're not guaranteed another look.' Or more simply, 'Pay attention to the beauty of God's world.'

We are reminded of the Imagist Movement of the early twentieth century (ca.1909–1917) founded by Ezra Pound. He was influenced by Asian poetry like the haiku, a poem that acutely focuses on physical details minus exposition: the image speaks for itself. Poets, therefore, were encouraged to zero in on one thing to describe in a haiku-like simplicity; thus, image and immediacy became the hallmarks of such verse, whose best exponents were poets like H.D., W.C. Williams, Amy Lowell, Ezra Pound, Richard Aldington and the sadly forgotten Adelaide Crapsey. Imagist poetry with its precise, sharply delineated image evokes a unified impression. Pound said, 'It is better to present one Image in a lifetime, than to produce voluminous work.'[6] Thus the Imagist poem is a new vision uncluttered by multiple poetic figures of speech or metaphysics: its beauty lies in the image itself, becoming clothed with whatever the reader imagines.

Merton can be described as an Imagist Photographer, zeroing in on one thing. We can almost hear his 'Ah!' to what is photographically attended to in the now moment, while at the same time he obeys Pound's dictum, 'Make it new,' presenting the beheld in a new manner, one unique to the beholder. Again, we are reminded of Christ's dictum, '"Behold the lilies of the field",'[7] a gentle command to us all to retrieve a childlike wonder, and this Merton achieved during his hermitage years. We need only gaze at Griffin's pictures of Merton with a camera: he is like a grinning child with a new, cherished toy, an Adam seeing the world as if for the first time.

Griffin's book also contains his own photographs of Merton living in his hermitage. We see spontaneous images of Merton lugging wood for the fireplace, starting the fire, reading a book before a blazing hearth; there are also candid photos of his face, often smiling, sometimes musing. There is a wonderful series of photos capturing Jacque Maritain's visit to Merton's hermitage. How touching it is to see Merton serving coffee to the elderly, ill philosopher – one who so greatly influenced Merton, his an early voice that 'sang' Merton into the church. One picture shows Merton sitting on the ground holding and examining his camera; his acute attention and gentle handling of the fine gift of a camera from Griffin is moving. Indeed the happiest photographs in the book are Griffin's photos of Merton holding his camera hanging from a strap around his neck, and on his face a huge smile. No doubt about it, photography brought great joy into Merton's life, and if he had lived longer it would surely have remained an important part of his life as an artist.

As mentioned, Merton's photographs are non-verbal, haiku-like images captured on film – images either deliberately arranged or inadvertently found, and swiftly photographed in a moment of 'Ah!'-ness when the beholder's ego disappears to capture the moment, demanding all of one's aesthetic sensibilities, talent, and discipline. The duration of a photograph is as swift as the click of a shutter, but it entails choice, angle, and light, the result of which can be one of manifold richness, perhaps capturing a world in a grain of sand or the world's beauty in a wild flower or the infinity of the heavens perceived through a screen of intertwining bare branches.

Crispin Sartwell's *Six Names of Beauty* is a profound meditation on the nature of the beautiful. The chapter 'Wabi-Sabi, Japanese, humility, imperfection' explores how the term *wabi-sabi* refers to an elusive and elegant beauty. *Wabi* is translated as 'poverty.' It connotes the life of farmers (peasants) tilling the land; back-breaking, simple, austere work – often a lonely life. Its aesthetic meaning implies ordinary, inexpensive tools that have aged from long use, wares that have become cracked, bent and worn. Such poor, lowly items mimic nature's declension: like falling leaves, soil erosion, grass in drought, decaying trees and fading blossoms. *Wabi*, therefore, suggests a beauty of elegant imperfection.

Sabi means loneliness or rather aloneness. It also refers to spar-seness and austerity. The Japanese flower arrangement best illus-trates its meaning: the idea that less is more with one flower attentively placed in a vase as opposed to a dozen flowers thoughtlessly dropped into one. Together, *wabi-sabi* suggests the beauty of 'the withered, weathered, tarnished, scarred, intimate, coarse, earthly, evanescent, tentative, ephemeral.'[8]

In order to comprehend *wabi-sabi* more fully, we should imagine a broken earthen cup next to an exquisite Royal Doulton porcelain cup, or a broken branch of autumn leaves next to a cluster of white lilies, or a wrinkled old woman next to a young, beautiful model, or a blunt pencil next to a Mont Blanc, or a faded, worn slipper next to an elegant Ferragamo loafer.

Sartwell's best example of *wabi-sabi* is the most famous tea bowl in the world: the Kizaemon tea bowl. It is a priceless but flawed Korean crockery of the sixteenth century. It is so asymmetrical, cracked and imperfect that one might fail to notice it; but it is an example *par excellence* of Japanese beauty, possessing the sine qua non of *wabi-sabi*: patina.

The *American Heritage Dictionary* defines patina as:

> 1. A thin layer of corrosion usually brown or green that appears on copper or copper alloys such as bronze, as a result of natural or artificial oxidation. 2. The sheen produced by age and use on any antique surface.[9]

The word patina derives from 'paten', which in Greek means dish. The bronze paten was used as the dish upon which rested the transubstantiated host, the body and blood of Christ. Patens were sacred objects, rarely thrown away; kept for generations, they gradually turned the mottled green we now call patina.

Which brings us back to Merton. His aesthetic sensibility possessed much that was Japanese. Esther de Waal's book, *A Seven Day Journey with Thomas Merton*, contains twenty of Merton's photographs. They are all stunning photos imbued with *wabi-sabi*: photographs of a chair, a bench and objects against a wall, a ladle and pan, a tree trunk, a well worn woodcutter's trestle, gnarled tree stumps and roots, a pock-marked stone, a striated rock and a small tree, a cross against the sky, the base of a wicker basket, trees in a meadow, a glove on a stool, a large metallic jug, a stone wall and a collection of bricks and mugs.

Some of these objects possess patina, or rather *wabi-sabi*. The 'glove on a stool' shows a used glove on a wooden stool that could have been made by Cistercians in the mid-nineteenth century. It also casts a substantial shadow, emphasizing not only its utilitarian solidity but its 'isness.' The pock-marked boulder possesses a strange beauty, suggesting eons of longevity as well as our own physical impermanence. The photograph of the ladle and pan is perhaps the best example of *wabi-sabi*: it is obviously old, its patina the result of monks' hands, its use likely begun at the founding of the abbey. Yet there they stand on the ground still useful, made by monks who understood and appreciated its value.

Another good example of *wabi-sabi* is the photograph of a large metallic jug. If we look closely, we can see its bumps, dents and bruises: it has obviously been much used. In its plainness, sitting on a sun-blazed wooden table, casting a shadow on the stone wall behind it, it is beautiful in its simplicity of form and purpose, as beautiful as Williams' wheelbarrow glazed in rain.

Let us return to John Howard Griffin. On Griffin's last visit to Merton, before Merton's journey to Asia, both Griffin and Merton spent the day photographing. Merton, he writes, became excited by everything he saw, 'the peeling paint on window facings, plants, weeds, the arrangement of a stack of wood chips. He would see something in the distance, wander away to photograph it from all angles, and then return.'[10] As Merton photographed, Griffin photographed him in the act of photographing, 'in which his joy was unblemished and which added a special aura of happiness to his features.'[11]

Then a sudden downpour drove them back to the abbey. Sitting in his rented car, Griffin watched Merton through rain-pocked windows as he walked up the path toward his hermitage, scrupulously careful to cover and protect his camera from the rain. We recall another image: Merton the little boy sitting in a rain-drenched car and gazing through a rain-scribbled window at his father entering a hospital for his final visit to his dying wife. Griffin, now in the place of the boy, observes Merton disappear – never again to see him.

Merton naturally took his camera to Asia where a faulty fan in his room electrocuted him as he was emerging wet from a shower. His body was returned on a plane carrying the corpses of American soldiers from Vietnam. John Howard Griffin was careful to request that the authorities not open Merton's camera since it might contain exposed film, and they kindly complied. After many weeks, the camera and lenses arrived at Griffin's home. He trembled so much he could not open it, so his wife did. Griffin was astonished to see how spotless the camera and lenses were, and looking at the frame counter, he saw that eighteen shots had been taken of a roll of thirty-six. Never before in his life had Griffin so scrupulously developed film, and he was overjoyed to find good, clean, crisp images. The first photograph to emerge was one taken from a height, a picture of the Bangkok River. And among those photographs is one of the Polonnaruwa Buddhas, where Merton had his most numinous spiritual experience.

Merton's attraction to the art of photography is not surprising. Photography is a solitary endeavour: one must be alone. One also needs silence. Solitude and silence are the sine qua non of being a contemplative. In fact, a photographer is a contemplative in his own right: he too must become a master of attention. Thus, in his own way he prays, again as Weil reminds us, 'Absolutely unmixed attention is prayer.'

Merton had in so many ways mastered attention, culminating during his years in his hermitage. Just as the mystic must dare to leap into divine darkness, the photographer must also take a leap of hope. There is at first the choice of subject, and then follow decisions of angle and light, but in the end when he clicks the camera's shutter, he is not absolutely certain of the results. He can only hope he has captured the moment's beauty. The physical and the camera's eye come together: eye, camera *and* object become one. We think of Emerson's famous religious experience in his essay 'Nature' – 'I become a transparent eyeball. I am nothing. I see all.' It is a statement not much different from Meister Eckhart's 'The eye with which I see God is the same eye with which God sees me.' Thus, when we are truly attentive, we lose ourselves only to find ourselves, the circular zero of eye and camera lens moving from nothing to Christ's promise of life more abundant, which is always among and within us.

At first glance, the black and white of Merton's calligraphy and photography may seem at opposite ends of the artistic spectrum. The calligrapher's movement is swift and spontaneous, its image instantly emerging for immediate appreciation. Such art entails surrendering to the unknown, allowing the hand and brush to go where it has (wants) to go without interference from ego or intellect.

Merton's photography, however, is a more deliberating act of attention: he must carefully hold the camera with its delicate glass eye, carefully choose his subjects as well as angles, taking into consideration light (as well as weather) before clicking the shutter; thus, photography is a slower artistic endeavor than the quicksilver strokes of calligraphy. The photographer outside taking pictures paradoxically ends up in the dark room, for until he views his developed film, he is unsure of the final product, uncertain whether or not he has succeeded in capturing the chosen image.

Therefore, there is risk involved in photography. Not only because one might fail at taking a fine photo but also because one may indeed produce one with the power to change our lives. Photography demands that we look with all our being. Think of Orpheus' turning to Eurydice and losing her; of Narcissus gazing at and falling in love with his own image, or the many who gazed upon the Medusa and turned into stone. These are the pagan warnings of the risks of looking.

Our cultural, religious admonitions are similar. Think of Lot's wife turning to look at Sodom and Gomorrah, and becoming a pillar of salt. Or those who gazed upon Christ and instantly fell in love with him, unquestionably obeying his summons, 'Come, follow me.' Consider Christ encouraging us to behold the lilies of the field, for he understood how a look can transform a life, for good or bad.

Thus, to gaze upon Merton's photographs can become a spiritual exercise, by offering them our complete undivided attention, they may indeed change us, teach us, inspire us, help us, like him, to retrieve a child's wonder, connecting us again with the world's beauty. Paying attention (looking) is a risk encouraged by the New Testament, for Christ uttered it long before Ezra Pound, 'I make all things new.' (Rev. 21:5.)

Because Merton called his camera 'a Zen camera,'[12] it is appropriate to end on a Zen note. The Japanese term *yugen* is a difficult one to translate into English: it is a combination of *sabi* and *wabi*: to 'form a still point of oceanic, calm and penetrating insight.'[13] It is so subtle a state of being that Zen writers are reluctant to describe it. But D.T. Suzuki, Merton's Zen mentor, takes the plunge: 'all great works of art embody in them *yugen* whereby we attain a glimpse of things eternal in the world of constant changes.'[14]

Merton's art, both his abstract calligraphy and his photography are imbued with *yugen*, offering us glimpses of a world less forlorn, one fraught with divine vestiges, if we would only make the effort to convert our eyes to pay attention and Look!

LOVE AND DO WHAT YOU WILL

To understand Merton's journey to love, it is helpful to look at it through the lens of Eliot's poem *The Love Song of J. Alfred Prufrock*; it is a fruitful exercise because not only does it shed light on Merton's love-thwarted life but also on his journey to a greater wholeness both as a man and as a Cistercian monk who is also an artist. First, let us revisit Prufrock.

Preparing for yet another tea party, Prufrock wonders:

> 'Do I dare?' and 'Do I dare?'
> Do I dare
> Disturb the universe?[1]

One's heart goes out to such a frightened person who yearns to connect with someone of the opposite sex: to connect and hopefully to fall in love. But Prufrock is terrified into silence and into inaction, like Eliot's paralysed hollow men. Prufrock's eyes, however, are ever moving, eyes ravenous to connect with the eyes of another, eyes that have not failed to notice the light brown hair on the women's arms, but his hunger for love is veiled and disguised by the shadow of his terror, not only of rejection but also of exposing his vulnerability.

So his unrequited longing renders Prufrock an old man, who in an enervated, dirge-like voice intones, 'I grow old ... I grow old ...' For a brief moment, he imagines himself as a nonchalant, free, brave and spontaneous young man, rakishly walking the beach with the bottoms of his trousers rolled up and his hair stylishly parted. He would like to eat a peach unselfconsciously, permitting the peach juice to trickle down his chin. But this occurs only in his imagination: he is much too afraid and painfully self-conscious ever to eat fruit in public.

Having perhaps personally known or privately observed such

fear and self-consciousness, we may smile at Prufrock's adolescent-like timidity. But I believe it is far deeper than a passing shyness: Prufrock is essentially afraid of life, too long succumbing to the syndrome of the unlived life. Such fear-haunted, wounded, enervated characters fill Henry James' novels; their most daring deed, like Prufrock's, is to balance a teacup upon their knees.

Henry James himself understood full well the dangers of the unlived life. Through one of his characters in his novel *The Ambassadors*, he pleads:

> Live all you can; it's a mistake not to. It doesn't so much matter what you do in particular, so long as you have your life. If you haven't had that what have you had? Do what you like so long as you don't make my mistake. Live![2]

How does Thomas Merton fit in with J. Alfred Prufrock? Unlike Prufrock, Merton lost his virginity at an early age. As a young man at Cambridge College, he fathered a child. He had many girl-friends and was obviously not intimidated by sexuality or the opposite sex. But I believe that he was very much afraid of love. For further elucidation, we must now return to Merton's journals.

Let us fast forward to Thomas Merton of 1966 when he was in his early 50s. He has already fallen in love with his nurse whom he refers to as M. On 15 April 1966, he writes in his journal:

> Love. I have got to dare to love, and bear the anxiety of self-question that love arouses in me, until 'perfect love casts out fear.'[3]

We hear the Prufrockian echo, 'Do I dare' and 'Do I dare, but contrary to the fear-dominated Prufrock, Merton finally chooses to love, a decision resonating with an Augustinian timbre, 'Love and do what you will.' It must have been an agonizing decision for a monk, also a priest, to accept his nurse's love and to return it. But for Merton it was clear-cut; either he dared to love or he would have to 'instinctively go back to the old routine of drawing into my shell and putting up the defenses, not letting it go any further, anticipating the break to make it easier for myself.'[4]

He also says, 'I see how badly I need her love to complete me with warmth and understanding and how utterly alone I am without her now. Some talk for a hermit! But it is true and I may as well admit it.'[5]

Note well Merton's fear of drawing back into his shell, and recall Prufrock's bleak and unsettling comparison of himself to a crustacean: 'Scuttling across the floors of silent seas.'[6]

What could be more distant on this earth than the bottom of the sea? What could be more lonely, trapped within a shell, removed from touching or being touched? I think of the poet Anne Sexton's announcement in *An Awful Rowing toward God* that, 'Touch is all.'[7]

Merton craves to touch and to be touched:

> I begin to seethe with physical desire, then become restless, disturbed, distressed, and fearful for the future.[8]

He sounds rather like a young man head-over-heels in love, one who has transcended his former fear and sense of unworthiness. He admits:

> By all standards it's all wrong, absurd insane … but somehow it is not crazy.[9]

Echoing Prufrock, he knows that to love a woman will disturb his universe, but it is a vital step along the way of his individuation, one necessitating an integration of the anima, the feminine archetype. In fact, Carl Jung suggests that if the encounter with the shadow is the 'apprentice-piece' of individuation, then coming to terms with the anima is the 'master-piece' of individuation.[10]

In Merton's *A Vow of Conversation*, we meet his dream anima figures: Proverb, the Lady Latinist, the Chinese Princess and the Black Mother. They all symbolically address what Merton has candidly described as his 'refusal of women.' These hauntingly eloquent dream figures clearly presage the appearance of his nurse, M. And, of course, there is the mystifyingly prophetic line from the haunting prose-poem 'Hagia Sophia':

> Such is the awakening of one man, one morning, at the voice of a nurse in the hospital. Awakening out of languor and

darkness, one of helpfulness, out of sleep, newly confronting reality and finding it to be gentleness.[11]

Prior to meeting his nurse, Merton had never experienced true love for a woman. We find in his journal this remarkable 23 June 1965 entry (note the reference to Eliot's *Four Quartets*):

> The other day … after my Mass I suddenly thought of Ann Winser, Andrew's little sister. She was about twelve or thirteen when I used to visit him on the Isle of Wight … She was the quietest thing on it, dark and secret child. One does not fall in love with a child of thirteen, and I hardly remember even thinking of her … Actually, I think she is a symbol of the true (quiet) woman I never really came to terms with in the world, and because of this there remains an incompleteness that cannot be remedied. When I came to the monastery, Ginny Burton was the symbol of the girl I ought to have fallen in love with but didn't (and she remains the image of one I really did love with a love of companionship not of passion).[12]

Ann Winser and Ginny Burton had over time become for Merton symbols of women. Anima dream figures and symbols can only direct attention toward one's incompleteness. (Notice also that Merton believed his incompleteness could never be 'remedied'.) Soul work on the conscious level must also be accomplished for healing to occur. How ironic that Merton, a writer who offered spiritual healing to so many readers through his books, was himself in dire need of healing. To borrow Henri Nouwen's phrase, he was truly a 'wounded healer' in search of healing.

For Merton to refuse M.'s love would be tantamount to saying 'No' to a greater psychic wholeness. He would remain as he describes himself: an incomplete man. However, he chooses to surrender himself to what he describes as the 'womanly wisdom in M. which instinctively seeks out the wound in me that most needs her sweetness, and lavishes all her love upon me there. Instead of feeling impure I feel purified.'[13]

The cerebral man finally and humbly bows before feeling — before the archetypal feminine.

Recall the woman of the gospel who breaks the alabaster jar and lovingly pours its perfume upon Christ's head. Merton's nurse breaks through to Merton, breaks the shell behind which he has hidden, and releases the love so long pent up, and she in turn pours upon him her own love. Love often entails a breaking, but more of that later.

During his relationship with M. we see Merton at his most vulnerable. Her love has stripped him of masks. That is not to say that Merton was deeply layered in masks, but he rarely appeared in his journals without wearing his writer's mask. He had always viewed his journals as works of art, and he surely knew full well that future scholars would mine them, but his journals were more than art. William Gass comments on inveterate diarists like Merton:

> Loneliness is the diary keeper's lover. It is not narcissism that takes them to their desk every day. The diary is demanding; it imposes its routine; it must be 'chored' the way one must milk a cow; and it alters your attitude toward life, which is lived, finally, only in order that it may make its way to the private page.[14]

We can imagine the blank page staring at Merton, commanding him to fill its white space with life, and Merton ever willing and happy to obey its summons. But there came a time when the diary's pure white page proved insufficient. A page cannot reach out to touch, it cannot love, it can only reflect back the solitary self.

In these spring and summer journal entries of 1966, Merton unselfconsciously expresses himself; he even dares to describe himself in love: love reduces him to a comic teenager; thus, Merton is not only in touch with his anima but also with the *puer aeternus*, the eternal boy archetype. And the added boon is that he is writing his most naked and disarming poetry, verse that is the antithesis of his obscure and opaque *The Geography of Lograire*.

Let us consider one of his *18 Poems:*

And God did not make death

I always obey my nurse
I always care

For wound and fracture
Because I am always broken
I obey my nurse

And God did not make death
He did not make pain
But the little blind fire
That leaps from one wound into another
Knitting the broken bones
And fixing sins so that they can be forgotten

I will obey my nurse who keeps this fire
Deep in her wounded breast
For God did not make death

He did not make pain
Or the arrogant wound
That smells under the official bandage

Because I am always broken I obey my nurse
Who in her grey eyes and her mortal breast
Holds an immortal love the wise have fractured
Because we have both been broken we can tell
God did not make death

I will obey the little spark
That flies from fracture to fracture
And the explosion
Where God did not make death
But only vision

I will obey my nurse's broken heart
Where all fires come from
And the abyss of flame
Knitting pain to pain
And the abyss of light
Made of pardoned sin
For God did not make death

I always obey the spark that smacks like lightning
In the giant night
I obey without question

The outlaw reasons
The cries in the abyss
From the world's body that the wise have fractured

For God did not make death
He did not make prisons
Or stalking canonical ravens
The dirt in the incision

I will obey my nurse
I will always take care
Of my fractured religion[15]

'I always obey my nurse' can be read as an analgesic for all the J. Alfred Prufrocks of the world. Or in Jungian terms, he obeys his anima and in order to do so he must disobey his vows and his abbot. Keep in mind that Merton for a lifetime obeyed masculine authority represented by his beloved father Owen Merton, his guardian Tom Bennett, his friend-mentors Robert Lax, Daniel Walsh and Mark Van Doren, his abbots, and of course, the patriarchal Rule of St Benedict. This pervading male dominance is the crux of Merton's spiritual and psychological dilemma: if there is to be a major transformation of consciousness in his life there must be a new birth, and without acceptance of the feminine principle there can be no rebirth. Therefore, 'I always obey my nurse' is Merton's minimalist *Apologia pro Vita Sua*, as well as a declaration of independence. What he clearly declares is that to anyone quick to judge him with disobedience, either of rule or vows, is wasting his breath. To become an integrated, whole human being, Merton *must* obey that for which he has for too long paid only intermittent attention: the feminine principle.

'I always obey my nurse' employs the word 'broken' five times, 'wound' four times, 'fractured' four times, 'pain' three times and 'death' seven times (a John Donne-like conceit for love's consummation?) The most repeated word in the poem is 'obey', used eight times. Today such a word as 'obey' or 'obedience' is rightly unpopular. It smacks of Uriah Heepish servility, fawning humility and low self-esteem, a word suggesting a disregard, if not contempt, for autonomy.

Ever aware of his monastic formation, Merton suggests that

obedience to his nurse is the wiser choice: the ego bows down to the anima in order to be raised in a greater life-giving, life-expanding consciousness, one that heals breaks and fractures and wounds, relieves pain and restores the patient to health and wholeness.

To obey implies listening: Merton first learns to listen to his nurse before obeying or rather choosing her. His decision is informed by what he hears but also by what he intuits his unconscious is demanding of him.

As a monk of Gethsemani, he had indeed listened to his anima, revealed most noticeably in his dreams of Proverb. Merton had begun a series of letters to his dream figure Proverb in 1958; the fruit of this encounter with Proverb was the famous Louisville Vision of 18 March 1958, a paean to universal acceptance and love of his brothers and sisters.

Merton experienced another encounter with the feminine archetype when he became entranced by Victor Hammer's painting of a young woman offering a crown to a young man. Merton allowed the beauty of Hammer's work and its theme to resonate within him, and the fruit of the encounter is Merton's poem 'Hagia Sophia,' a poem extolling the utter importance of the feminine principle in life. Just before he completed his poem, Merton wrote to Victor Hammer (and included his commentary within his poem):

> The feminine principle in the universe is the inexhaustible source of creative realization of the Father's glory in the world and is in fact the manifestation of his glory...[16]

Merton and his nurse, both wounded in their unique ways, offer healing to each other. In this relationship, Merton's former 'refusal of women' transforms into an acceptance of women, or more accurately into the exquisite risk of love.

Now let us make a huge leap forward to Merton's trip to Asia. He is now standing before the Polonnaruwa Buddhas:

> I am able to approach the Buddhas barefoot and undisturbed, my feet in wet grass, wet sand. Then the silence of the extraordinary faces. The great smiles. Huge and yet subtle.

Filled with every possibility, questioning nothing, knowing everything, rejecting nothing, the peace not of emotional resignation but of Madhyamike, of sunyata, that has seen through every question without trying to discredit anyone or anything – *without refutation* – without establishing some other argument. For the doctrinaire, the mind that needs well-established positions, such peace, such silence, can be frightening. I was knocked over with a rush of relief and thankfulness at the obvious clarity of the figures, the clarity and fluidity of shape and line, the design of the monumental bodies composed into the rock shape and landscape, figure, rock and tree. And the sweep of bare rock sloping away on the other side of the hollow, where you can go back and see different aspects of the figures.[17]

Merton's beholding of these Buddhas is an exquisite act of attention to Beauty, as well as an acceptance of the wisdom that God is the source of all beauty. Gazing upon the Polonnaruwa Buddhas is simultaneously an aesthetic experience as well as a deeply religious one. Notice that this son of a father who painted like Cézanne renders a rather astute, artistic evaluation of the Buddhas: he comments on their clarity, fluidity of shape, line and design and gazes upon the Buddhas from different aspects and angles. He is here very much himself the connoisseur of the beautiful. But then there is the sudden loss of ego:

Looking at these figures I was suddenly, almost forcibly, jerked clean out of the habitual, half-tied vision of things, and an inner clearness, clarity, as if exploding from the rocks themselves became evident and obvious. The thing about all this is that there is no puzzle, no problem, and really no 'mystery.' All problems are resolved and everything is clear, simply because what matters is clear ... I don't know what else remains but I have now seen and have pierced through the surface and have got beyond the shadow and the disguise.[18]

To more deeply comprehend what happened to Merton in that egoless moment, let us first look at it as an aesthetic experience.

What happens when great art takes your breath away (and I might add, your ego)? Ken Wilbur writes:

> Great art suspends the reverted eye, the lamented past, the anticipated future: we enter with it into the timeless present: we are with God today, perfect in our manner and mode, open to the riches and the glories of a realm that time forgot, but that great art reminds us of: not by its content, but by what it does in us: suspends the desire to be elsewhere. And maybe for a second, maybe for a minute, maybe for all eternity – releases us from the coil of ourselves.
>
> That is exactly the state that great art pulls us into, no matter what the actual content of the art itself – bugs, or Buddhas, landscapes or abstractions, it doesn't matter in the least ... great art is judged by its capacity to take your breath away, take your self away, take time away, all at once.[19]

Keep in mind that the journal entry that records and describes Merton's aesthetic illumination before the Polonnaruwa Buddhas was written after the fact. Writing in his journal, he is looking back upon an overwhelming experience, likely struggling to find the most exact words to describe what is essentially indescribable. I think of Wallace Stevens in his poem *Thirteen Ways of Looking at a Blackbird*. He writes:

> I do not know which to prefer,
> The beauty of inflections,
> Or the beauty of innuendos,
> The blackbird whistling
> Or just after.[20]

Merton's experience is beautiful but so is his prose description of it.

Let us look at his experience from a Jungian perspective. Although I cannot prove it definitively, I believe that Merton's nurse *enabled* Merton to experience this extraordinary event in his life: it is the fruit of their relationship, as was the Louisville Vision and 'Hagia Sophia' the fruit of his dream figure Proverb. Or one can simply say that Merton's whole life paved the way for this aesthetic illumination, and if we accept this, then an elimination of any life event, small or momentous, could jeopardize his last, and perhaps greatest, illumination, so even from this perspective his love affair with his nurse remains vitally important.

The Cistercian monk who stood without shoes before the Buddhas was the broken man healed, restored and made whole by his nurse so that with eyes cleansed by love, he could gaze upon the Buddhas and lose himself in Beauty, illustrating Christ's dictum: in losing yourself you will find yourself.

There are several other ways by which we can understand what Merton experienced before the Polonnaruwa Buddhas. We could describe it as simply a Henry Jamesian moment of beauty, or a Virginia Woolfian moment of being, or a Simone Weilian moment of exquisite attention during which the ego disappears and the observer and the observed become one. Simone Weil's concept is appealing to me because she says that 'absolutely unmixed attention is prayer,' and I believe that when Merton stood before the Buddhas he had entered a contemplative moment that was true prayer. But to comprehend the depth and profundity of Merton's experience, we are wise again to turn to T.S. Eliot, particularly his concept of the 'still point,' for it appears that Merton had pierced through temporality to timelessness, which to comprehend fully is, as Eliot would say, 'an occupation for a saint.' Our only qualification is that rather than use the restrictive word 'saint' let us employ instead the expression 'holy person;' thus, what Merton experienced is potentially an occupation for all of us.

Let us now leap backwards to the 1939 World's Fair art exhibit. We recall that several paintings catch Merton's eye; one of them is Pieter Bruegel's *The Wedding Dance*. As previously mentioned, it is one of wild celebration with people drinking, dancing, flirting and generally having a grand time. Merton's reaction to the subject of the painting, however, is negatively critical: he sees these characters celebrating a wedding as miserable people escaping their mundane lives by drunkenness and lascivious behaviour. His response is a case of psychological projection by an earthy young man manifesting an early *contemptus mundi*. While looking at Bruegel, he shifts his gaze to a small figure of a man at the top of the painting. Let us again review it:

One, rigid, solitary, little man in grey with his back to the whole business, simply looking away at nothing, off at the back and top of the picture. He is paying no attention to anything, doing nothing, just standing, ignoring everything of the subject matter, and yet being an essential element in the construction of the whole picture.[21]

What a prophetic piece of writing! Like the wedding guest, he will seemingly turn his back on the world. And this rejection of the world will last for a time. It is our belief, however, that Merton's dream anima figures helped him to turn back towards the world, towards people with all their flaws and virtues – and when he looked, he did so with eyes of compassion. Thus the inner gaze transforms itself into an outward gaze, a transformation that should take place in the lives of all contemplatives, for there is always the danger of the inner journey dead-ending in a trap of narcissism.

Many years later his hospital nurse, who fell in love with him and he with her, invites him into the dance of life. And he says 'yes' to the dance and for a brief time he is a happy member of the wedding party. But he gradually realizes, as he admits to M. in his 'Midsummer journal', that this life is not for him. His way is a solitary one, not to be graced with marriage and family. Such is his destiny, and he obeys it as he once obeyed his nurse.

Let us now fast-forward to Asia. It is generally agreed that Merton's epiphany in Sri Lanka is his most numinous mystical experience. I use the word numinous as Rudolph Otto defines it in his book, *The Idea of the Holy*. Otto well understood the sublime power of Oriental art to express the numinous. Quoting Oswald Siren commenting on the Lung-Men Buddha, Otto says:

Anyone who approaches this figure will realize that it has a religious significance without knowing anything about its *motif* … It matters little whether we call it a prophet or a god, because it is a complete work of art permeated by a spiritual will, which communicates itself to the beholder … The religious element of such a figure is immanent; it is a 'presence' or an atmosphere rather than a formulated idea … it cannot be described in words, because it lies beyond intellectual definition.[22]

Some Christians are puzzled, a few actually disturbed, that Merton's seemingly most numinous epiphany occurred in the East before the great, stone Buddhas and not in the West in a specifically Christian ambience, like a church or a Gothic cathedral, or before a painting by one of our great Christian masters. Even the staid, conservative, unemotional T.S. Eliot himself fell to his knees when he first gazed upon Michaelangelo's *Pietà*. But for Merton it would be the Buddhas that took his breath away. The Jesuit William Johnston finds nothing contradictory for a Christian to be overwhelmed by the numinous of the East; he writes:

> The question usually asked, however, is: 'What about the role of Christ?' Or, as someone facetiously put it, 'Do you leave Christ at the door of the temple with your shoes?'
>
> And to this I would answer with Paul that no authentic Christian can be separated from the love of Christ. If he enters the Buddhist temple, he does so as a member of Christ – to grow in the Christ experience and to search for Christ who, he believes, is there in another way.[23]

When he embarked upon his trip to Asia, Merton admitted to still being a pilgrim seeking the door leading to wisdom. In one of his very last journal entries, he meditates on the various doors to wisdom:

> The door without wish. The undesired. The unplanned door. The door never expected. Not select. Not exclusive. Not for a few. Not for many. Not *for*. Door without aim. Door without end. Does not respond to a key – so do not imagine you have a key. Do not have your hopes on possession of the key.[24]

Later, he completes his meditation, saying:

> Christ said, 'I am the door.' The nailed door. The cross, they nail the door shut with death. The resurrection: 'You see, I am not a door ... I am the opening, the "shewing," the revelation, the door of light, the Light itself. "I am the Light,"' and the light is in the world from the beginning.[25]

Just as Merton needed M. to complete him as a man through a psychological recognition and acceptance of life's feminine principle, he also needed a spiritual marriage of opposites: of East and West. Like another religious who turned to the East, Bede Griffiths (1906–93), Merton went to India 'to find the other half of his soul – the intuitive, contemplative dimension that is much neglected in the West but richly present in traditional India.'[26] Merton intuitively understood that Western Christianity, like the Western world, is lopsided and overly patriarcal and desperately needs India's reverence of the feminine principle.

Pieter Bruegel, Proverb, the anima dream figures, his nurse M. and his final trip to Asia: all are emblematic of a pilgrim's search for feminine wisdom: 'Hagia Sophia.'

That Merton was granted, in T.S. Eliot's phrase, 'a tremor of bliss, a wink of heaven, a whisper'[27] on 2 December 1968 is certain. It is not for us to grasp the complete meaning of what happened to this modern, holy pilgrim, for to do so is like grasping water. I believe, however, that we must not cease to explore the meaning, as Eliot would advise. And who knows, by a combination of attention and grace, we too may be jerked clean out of the habitual, half-tied vision of things and perhaps for the first time see beyond the shadow and the disguise.

ENDNOTES

Introduction

1. Simone Weil, *Gravity and Grace*, introduction by Gustave Thibon and Thomas R. Nevin (Nebraska, University of Nebraska, 1997), p. 170.
2. Simone Weil, *The Simone Weil Reader*, ed. George A. Panichas (New York, David McKay Company, Inc., 1977), p. 44.
3. 'Czeslaw Milosz on Merton', *Merton Journal*, Advent 2004, vol. II, no. 2, p. 4.
4. Thomas Merton, *The Seven Storey Mountain* (New York, Harcourt, Brace & Co., 1948), p. 109.
5. Weil, *Simone Weil Reader*, p. 15.
6. ibid., p. 379.
7. ibid., p. 52.
8. ibid.
9. Thomas Merton, *The Hidden Ground of Love: Letters of Religious Experience and Social Concerns*, ed. William Shannon (New York, Farrar, Straus, Giroux, 1985), p. 376.
10. Thomas Merton, *Raids on the Unspeakable* (New York, New Directions, 1964), p. 181.

Biography

1. Thomas Merton, *The Silent Life* (New York, Farrar, Straus, & Cudahy, 1957), pp. 21–3.
2. Thomas Merton, *Conjectures of a Guilty Bystander* (New York, Doubleday, 1966), p. 140.
3. Thomas Merton, *The Asian Journal of Thomas Merton* (New York. A New Directions Book, 1968), p. 233.
4. Thomas Merton, *Contemplation in a World of Action* (Notre Dame, University of Notre Dame Press, 1998), p. 206.

The Connoisseur of Beauty

1. Thomas Merton, *The Seven Storey Mountain* (New York, Harcourt, Brace & Co., 1948), p. 83.
2. ibid.

3. ibid., pp. 108–9.
4. Thomas Merton, *Seeds of Contemplation* (New York, New Directions, 1961), p. 17.
5. Merton, *Seven Storey Mountain*, p. 110.
6. Simone Weil, *Simone Weil Reader*, ed. George A. Panichas (New York, David McKay, 1977), p. 474.
7. Thomas Merton, *No Man is an Island* (New York, Harcourt, Brace, Jovanovich, 1978), p. 34.
8. John Navone, *Enjoying God's Beauty* (Collegeville, The Liturgical Press, 1999), p. 9.
9. Weil, *Simone Weil Reader*, p. 473.
10. Merton, *Seven Storey Mountain*, p.111.
11. Walter Hilton, *The Scale of Perfection* (London, Geoffrey Chapman, 1975), quoted in J.M. Cohen and J.F. Phipps, *The Common Experience* (New York, St Martin's Press, 1979), p. 145.
12. Merton, *Seven Storey Mountain*, p. 111.
13. F.C. Happold, *Mysticism: a Study and an Anthology* (London, Penguin Books, 1963), p. 73.:14.
14. Thomas Merton, *Run to the Mountain: The Story of a Vocation. The Journals of Thomas Merton, Vol. 1: 1939–1941*, ed. Patrick Hart OCSO (San Francisco, HarperSanFrancisco, 1995), p. 53.
15. Simone Weil, *Waiting for God* (New York, HarperCollins, First Perennial, 2001), p. xxxi.
16. Weil, *Simone Weil Reader*, p. 477.
17. Merton, *Run to the Mountain*, p. 53.
18. Simone Weil, *Simone Weil: An Anthology*, ed. Siân Miles (New York, Grove Press, 1986), p. 212.
19. Weil, *Simone Weil Reader*, p. 45.
20. Weil, *Simone Weil Reader,* back cover blurb.
21. Merton, *Run to the Mountain*, p. 53.
22. ibid., p. 54.
23. ibid.
24. ibid., p. 56.
25. ibid., p. 272.
26. ibid., p. 87.
27. Thomas Merton, *No Man is an Island* (New York, Harcourt, Brace, Jovanovich, 1978), p. 33.
28. Francine Du Plessix Gray, *Simone Weil* (New York, Penguin, 2001), p. 120.

The Close Reader of Logos

1. Thomas Merton, *The Seven Storey Mountain* (New York, Harcourt, Brace & Co., 1948), pp. 85–6.

2. ibid., p. 86.
3. John Navone, *Enjoying God's Beauty* (Collegeville, The Liturgical Press, 1999), p. 57.
4. Patrick Henry (ed.), *Benedict's Dharma: Buddhists reflect on the Rule of Saint Benedict*, afterword by David Steindl-Rast OSB (New York, Riverhead Books, 2001), p. 194.
5. Michael Casey, *Sacred Reading: the ancient art of Lectio Divina* (Ligouri, Liguori/Triumph, 1996), p. 83.
6. Thomas Merton, *The Sign of Jonas: the Journal of Thomas Merton* (New York, Harcourt, Brace & Co., 1953), p. 165.
7. Thomas Merton, *Run to the Mountain: The Story of a Vocation. The Journals of Thomas Merton, Vol. 1: 1939–1941,* ed. Patrick Hart OCSO (San Francisco, HarperSanFrancisco, 1995), p. 258.
8. ibid.
9. Simone Weil, *The Simone Weil Reader*, ed. George A. Panichas (New York, David McKay, 1977), p. 45.
10. Merton, *The Sign of Jonas*, p. 165.
11. ibid., p. 191.
12. ibid., p. 186.
13. ibid., p. 193.
14. ibid., p. 195.
15. ibid., p. 213.
16. ibid., p. 215.
17. Theodore Roethke, 'On identity' in *On the Poet and His Craft* (Washington, University of Washington Press, 1966), p. 26.
18. Merton, *The Sign of Jonas*, p. 238.
19. ibid., pp. 95–6.
20. Thomas Merton, *New Seeds of Contemplation* (New York, New Directions, 1961), p. 34.
21. Barth, 'The sacramental vision of Gerard Manley Hopkins', pp. 289–90.
22. Merton, *The Sign of Jonas*, p. 238.
23. Weil, *Simone Weil Reader*, p. 378.
24. ibid., p. 423.
25. ibid., p. 469.
26. Merton, *The Sign of Jonas*, p. 69.
27. ibid., p. 274.
28. ibid., p. 275.
29. ibid.
30. ibid.
31. Mary Oliver, *White Pine* (New York, Harcourt, Brace and Co., 1991), p. 8.

The Merton, Weil and Milosz Connection

1. Thomas Merton, *Thomas Merton on Peace* (New York, The McCall Publishing Company, 1971), p. 144.
2. Thomas Merton, *Conjectures of a Guilty Bystander* (Garden City, Doubleday & Co., 1966), p. 305.
3. Thomas Merton, *A Vow of Conversation* (New York, Farrar, Straus, Giroux, 1988), p. 156.
4. Merton, *Vow,* p. 157.
5. ibid., p. 157.
6. Thomas Merton, *The Literary Essays of Thomas Merton* (New York, New Directions, 1981), p. 364.
7. Camille Paglia, *Break, Blow, Burn: Camile Paglia reads forty-three of the world's best poems* (New York, Pantheon Books, 2005), pp. 45–6.
8. Thomas Merton, *Thomas Merton on Peace*, ed. Gordon C. Zahn (New York, The McCall Publishing Company, 1971), p. 145.
9. Thomas Merton, *Entering the Silence: Becoming a Monk and Writer. The Journals of Thomas Merton, Vol. 2: 1941–1952*, ed. Jonathan Montaldo (San Francisco, HarperSanFrancisco, 1996), pp. 74–5.
10. Thomas Merton, *Thoughts in Solitude* (New York, Farrar, Straus, & Cudahy, 1958), p. 83.
11. Thomas Merton, *The Hidden Ground of Love: the Letters of Thomas Merton on Religious Experience and Social Concerns*, ed. William Shannon (New York, Farrar, Straus, Giroux, 1985), p. 376.
12. Thomas Merton, *The Courage for Truth: Letters to Writers* (New York, Farrar, Straus, Giroux), 1993, p. 59.
13. Thomas Merton, *Striving Towards Being: the Letters of Thomas Merton and Czeslaw Milosz*, ed. Robert Faggen (New York, Farrar, Straus, Giroux, 1997), p. 75.
14. Czeslaw Milosz, *To Begin Where I Am: Selected essays* (New York, Farrar, Straus, Giroux, 2001), p. 259.
15. Merton, *Vow,* p. 159.
16. Merton, *Seven Storey Mountain*, p. 401.
17. Weil, *Simone Weil Reader*, p. 15.
18. ibid., pp. 14–15.
19. Milosz, *To Begin Where I Am*, p. 250.
20. Weil, *Simone Weil Reader*, p. 49.
21. John C.H. Wu, *The Golden Age of Zen,* introduction by Thomas Merton (New York, Image Books, 1996), p. 16.
22. Merton, *Vow,* p. 189.
23. Simone Weil, *Simone Weil: An Anthology,* ed. Siân Miles (New York, Grove Press, 1986), p. 253.
24. Interview with Dr Jacques Cabaud, Simone Weil's first biographer,

speaking to Lyn Gallacher from his home in Germany, *Encounter* (ABC Radio National), 7 May 2000.

Alone with the Alone

1. Thomas Merton, *A Vow of Conversation* (New York, Farrar, Straus, Giroux, 1988), p. 53.
2. Rainer Maria Rilke, *Selected Letters: 1902–1926*, trans. R.F.C. Hull (New York, Quartet Books, 1988), p. 105.
3. Merton, *Vow*, p. 3.
4. Robinson Jeffers, *Rock and Hawk: A Selection of Shorter Poems* (New York, Random House, 1987), p. 218.
5. Merton, *Vow*, p. 11.
6. ibid., p. 18.
7. ibid., p. 45.
8. ibid., p. 93.
9. ibid.
10. ibid., p. 179.
11. ibid., p. 185.
12. ibid., p. 206.
13. ibid., p. 200.
14. Rainer Maria Rilke, *The Book of Hours: Prayers to a Lowly God*, trans. and with introduction by Annemarie S. Kidder (Evanston, Northwestern University Press, 2001), p. xix.
15. Merton, *Vow*, p. 165.
16. ibid., pp. 31–2.
17. ibid., pp. 43–4.
18. Luke 17:21b (King James Version).
19. Luke:17:21b (New Revised Standard Version).
20. Bede Griffiths, *The Golden String* (Springfield, Templegate Publishers, 1954), p. 9.
21. Merton, *Vow*, p. 174.
22. ibid., p. 44.
23. Aldous Huxley, *The Doors of Perception* (London, Chatto & Windus, 1954), pp. 11–12.
24. Thomas Merton, *Hidden Ground of Love*, ed. William Shannon (New York, Farrar, Straus, Giroux, 1985), p. 438.
25. Merton, *Vow*, p. 116.
26. ibid., p. 119.
27. ibid., p. 120.
28. ibid., p, 130.
29. ibid.
30. Laura Sewall, *Sight and Sensibility* (New York, Jeremy P. Tarcher, Putnam, 1999), pp. 32–3.

31. J. Neville Ward, *The Use of Prayer* (New York, Oxford University Press, 1977), p. 33.
32. D.T. Suzuki, *The Zen Doctrine of No Mind* (Maine, Samuel Weiser, 1969), p. 29.
33. Merton, *Vow*, p. 188.
34. ibid., p. 200.
35. ibid., p. 204.
36. ibid., pp. 207–8.
37. ibid. p. x.

The Abstract Calligraphist

1. Thomas Merton, *The Road to Joy: Letters to New and Old Friends*, selected and ed. Robert E. Daggy (New York, Farrar, Straus, Giroux, 1989), p. 281.
2. Thomas Merton, *A Vow of Conversation: Journals 1964–1965,* ed. Naomi Burton Stone (New York, Farrar, Straus, Giroux, 1988), p. 8.
3. Roger Lipsey, *Angelic Mistakes: the art of Thomas Merton* (Boston, New Seeds, 2006), p. 19.
4. Merton, *Vow*, p. 46.
5. Samuel Beckett, *Molloy*, trans. Beckett and Patrick Bowles (New York, Grove Press, 1955), p. 55.
6. Merton, *Vow*, p. 72.
7. ibid., p. 73.
8. Matti Megged, *Dialogue in the Void: Beckett & Giacometti* (New York, Lumen Books), 1985, p. 5.
9. Matthew 6:28 (King James Version).
10. Merton, *Vow*, p. 13.
11. ibid., p. 55.
12. Thomas Merton, *Raids on the Unspeakable* (New York, New Directions, 1964), p. 182.
13. Rainer Crone and Joseph Leo Koerner, *Paul Klee: Legends of the Sign* (New York, Columbia University Press, 1991), back cover.
14. Thomas Merton, *Raids on the Unspeakable* (New York, New Directions, 1964), pp. 180–81.
15. Merton, *Vow*, p. 61.
16. ibid., p. 65.
17. ibid., p. 89.
18. ibid., p. 94.
19. ibid., p. 110.
20. ibid., p. 105.

The Camera and the Contemplative Eye

1. Michael Mott, *The Seven Mountains of Thomas Merton* (Boston, Houghton Mifflin Company, 1986), p. 344.
2. ibid.
3. John Howard Griffin, *A Hidden Wholeness: the visual world of Thomas Merton* (Boston, Houghton Mifflin Company, 1970), p. 91.
4. ibid.
5. Wallace Stevens, *The Palm at the End of the Mind: Selected Poems and a Play*, ed. Holly Stevens (New York, Alfred A. Knopf, 1984), p. 54.
6. Herbert Read, *Form in Modern Poetry* (London, Vision Press, 1953), p. 74.
7. Matthew 6:28 (King James Version).
8. Crispin Sartwell, *Six Names of Beauty* (New York, Routlege, 2004), p. 114.
9. *The American Heritage Dictionary, Second College Edition* (Boston: Houghton Mifflin Company, 1991).
10. Esther de Waal, *A Seven Day Journey with Thomas Merton* (Ann Arbor, Servant Publications, 1992).
11. Griffin, *Hidden Wholeness*, p. 92.
12. Mott, *Seven Mountains*, p. 516.
13. John A. Rudy, *Wordsworth and the Zen Mind: the poetry of self-emptying* (New York, State University of New York State, 1996), p. 149.
14. ibid., p. 149.

Love and Do What You Will

1. T.S. Eliot, *The Complete Poems and Plays: 1909–1950* (New York, Harcourt, Brace, Jovanovich, 1980), pp. 4–5.
2. Henry James, *The Ambassadors* (Kanemann, 1996).
3. Thomas Merton, *Learning to Love: Exploring Solitude and Freedom,* ed. Christine M. Bochen, The Journals of Thomas Merton, vol. 6: 1966–1967 (San Francisco, HarperSanFrancisco, 1997), p. 44.
4. Merton, *Learning to Love*, p. 47.
5. ibid., p. 47.
6. Eliot, *The Complete Poems and Plays*, p. 5.
7. Anne Sexton, *The Awful Rowing Toward God* (Boston, Houghton Mifflin Company, 1975), p. 1.
8. Merton, *Learning to Love*, p. 48.
9. ibid., p. 50.
10. Daryl Sharp, *C.G. Jung Lexicon: A Primer of Terms and Concepts* (Toronto, Inner City Books, 1991), p. 22.
11. Thomas Merton, *In the Dark Before Dawn: New and Selected Poems of*

Thomas Merton, ed. Lynn R. Szabo (New York, New Directions, 2005), p. 66.

12. Thomas Merton, *Dancing in the Water of Life: Seeking Peace in the Hermitage. The Journals of Thomas Merton, Vol. 5: 1963–1965*, ed. Robert E. Daggy (San Francisco, HarperSanFrancisco, 1997), p. 259.

13. Merton, *Learning to Love*, p. 66.

14. William Gass, *A Temple of Texts* (New York, Alfred A. Knopf, 2006), p. 35.

15. Thomas Merton, *New Selected Poems of Thomas Merton*, ed. Lynn R. Szabo (New York, New Directions, 2005), p. 194.

16. Thomas Merton, *The Other Side of the Mountain: The End of the Journey. The Journals of Thomas Merton, Vol. 7: 1967–1968*, ed. Patrick Hart ocso, (San Francisco, HarperSanFrancisco), p. 323.

17. ibid., p. 324.

18. ibid.

19. Ken Wilbur, *The Eye of Spirit* (Boston. Shambhala, 1997), p 136.

20. Wallace Stevens, *The Palm at the End of the Mind*, ed. Holly Stevens, (Hamden, Archon Books, 1984), p. 20.

21. Thomas Merton, *Run to the Mountain: The Story of a Vocation. The Journals of Thomas Merton Vol. 1:1939–1941* ed. Patrick Hart, ocso, (SanFrancisco, 1995), p. 54.

22. Rudolph Otto, *The Idea of the Holy* (London, Oxford University Press, 1923), p. 67.

23. William Johnston, *The Inner Eye of Love*, (New York, Harper and Row, 1978), p. 86.

24. Merton, *Other Side of the Mountain*, p. 285.

25. ibid.

26. William Johnston, *Arise My Love: Mysticism for a New Era* (Maryknoll, Orbis Books, 2000), p. 70.

27. T.S. Eliot, 'Murder in the Cathedral', *The Complete Poems and Plays, 1909–1950* (New York, Harcourt Brace Jovanovich, Publishers, 1950), p. 209.